DUTCH OVEN BREAD COOKBOOK

Recipes for Basic, Spiced, Grain, Seed, Nut, Cheesy, Fruit, Veggie, Sweet, Sourdough & Holiday Breads.

Serena Rose

DUTCH OVEN BREAD COOKBOOK

A Beginner's Guide to Baking 100 Types of Bread at Home with Recipes for Basic, Spiced, Grain, Seed, Nut, Cheesy, Fruit, Veggie, Sweet, Sourdough & Holiday Breads

TABLE OF CONTENTS

INTRODUCTION	**5**
ALL ABOUT DUTCH OVEN BREAD BAKING	**6**
What is a Dutch Oven?	6
Advantages of Dutch Ovens in Bread Baking	6
Key Features for the Best Dutch Ovens for Bread	6
Baking Tips & Tricks for Dutch Oven Bread	6
Care and Maintenance of Dutch Ovens	7
DUTCH OVEN SIZES AND CAPACITIES TABLE	**7**
DRY MEASURE TABLE	**7**
LIQUID MEASURE TABLE	**8**
KITCHEN MEASUREMENT ABBREVIATIONS (STANDARD AND METRIC) TABLE	**8**
BASIC BREADS	**9**
1. Artisan Bread	9
2. Beer Bread	9
3. Ciabatta Bread	10
4. Crusty No-Knead Bread	10
5. Garlic Bread	10
6. Honey Oat Bread	11
7. Monkey Bread	11
8. No-Knead Cinnamon and Raisin Bread	12
9. No-Knead Whole Wheat Bread	12
10. Oatmeal Bread	12
11. Rustic French Bread	13
12. Soda Bread	13
13. White Bread	13
14. Whole Wheat Bread	14
15. Yeast Bread	14
SPICES AND HERB BREAD	**15**
16. Cheddar-Dill Bread	15
17. Cinnamon Raisin Bread	15
18. Garlic and Herb	16
19. Italian Herbs and Cheese No-Knead Bread	16
20. No-Knead Garlic Herb Bread	17
21. No-Knead Rosemary Parmesan Bread	17
22. Olive Oil & Italian Herb Bread	18
23. Rosemary Bread	18
24. Rosemary Parmesan Bread	19
25. Rosemary Thyme No-Knead Bread	19
26. Rustic Herb Loaf	20
27. Sun-Dried Tomato Basil No Knead Bread	20
28. Tomato and Olive Focaccia	21
GRAIN, SEED, AND NUTS BREADS	**21**
29. Cranberry Walnut Bread	21
30. Cranberry, Chia Seed & Almond No Knead Bread	22
31. Mulitseed No-Knead Bread	22
32. Multigrain Bread	22
33. No Knead Bread with Seeds	23
34. No Knead Fruit and Nut Bread	24
35. No Knead Quinoa Bread	24
36. Poppy Seed Bread	25
37. Pumpkin Seed Bread	25
38. Raisin Walnut Bread	25
39. Yogurt Flaxseed Bread	26
CHEESY BREADS	**26**
40. Artisan Ham & Cheese Bread	26
41. Cheddar Sage Bread	27
42. Cheesy Herb Artisan Bread	27
43. Cheesy Italian Bread	28
44. Cheesy Pull Apart Garlic Bread	28
45. Jalapeno Cheddar	29
46. No Knead Cheddar Bread	29
47. No Knead Cheese Bread	30
48. Rosemary Cheese Bread	30
49. Smoky Pepper Bread	31
FRUIT BREADS	**31**
50. Apple Yeast Bread	31
51. Banana Bread	32
52. Blueberry Bread	32
53. Cherry Walnut Loaf	33
54. Cranberry Orange Bread	33
55. No Knead Fruit Bread	34
56. Cranberry Pistachio Bread	34

57. CRUSTY APPLE CRANBERRY	35
58. LEMON BREAD WITH WILD BLUEBERRIES	35
59. NO KNEAD FIG AND WALNUT BREAD	36
60. NO-KNEAD CRANBERRY BREAD	36
61. NO-KNEAD VEGAN CRANBERRY ORANGE BREAD	37
62. PEAR, WALNUT & ROSEMARY BREAD	37
63. PUMPKIN BREAD	38

VEGETABLE BREADS — 38

64. CHEDDAR POTATO BREAD	38
65. NO KNEAD POTATO BREAD	39
66. ONION YEAST BREAD	39
67. SWEET POTATO BREAD	40
68. TOMATO BASIL BREAD	40
69. ZUCCHINI BREAD	41

SWEET BREADS — 41

70. CINNAMON MONKEY BREAD	41
71. DOUBLE CHOCOLATE NO-KNEAD BREAD	41
72. HONEY OAT ARTISAN BREAD	42
73. NO-KNEAD CHOCOLATE CHIP BREAD	42
74. NO-KNEAD CRANBERRY PECAN BREAD	43
75. NO-KNEAD SWEET CINNAMON BREAD	43
76. SWEET HONEY CORNBREAD	43

SOURDOUGH BREADS — 44

77. BEETROOT SOURDOUGH BREAD	44
78. CARROT RAISIN SOURDOUGH BREAD	44
79. COCOA CHOCOLATE CHERRY SOURDOUGH BREAD	45
80. CHERRY SEEDED SOURDOUGH BREAD	46
81. CHOCOLATE-CHERRY SOURDOUGH BREAD	47
82. HONEY, BLUE CHEESE AND WALNUT SOURDOUGH	47
83. LEMON BLUEBERRY SOURDOUGH BREAD	48
84. RASPBERRY WHITE CHOCOLATE SOURDOUGH BREAD	49
85. SOURDOUGH BREAD	50
86. SOURDOUGH BREAD WITH FLAX SEEDS	51
87. SOURDOUGH MAPLE PECAN HARVEST BREAD	52
88. SOURDOUGH ROSEMARY BREAD	53

HOLIDAYS BREADS — 53

89. BAGEL	53
90. BAGUETTE	54
91. BRAIDED SAFFRON CHALLAH BREAD	55
92. COCONUT & LIME BRIOCHE BUNS	55
93. CORNBREAD WITH GREEN CHILES	56
94. EGGNOG BREAD	56
95. NAAN	57
96. NO KNEAD CINNAMON SWIRL BREAD	57
97. OLIVE OIL AND ROSEMARY NO KNEAD BREAD	58
98. PANETTONE	58
99. PITA BREAD	59
100. ROSCA DE REYES	60

INTRODUCTION

There's something magical about the aroma of freshly baked bread, just out of the oven with a crackling crust and soft, pillowy interior. Baking hearty, wholesome loaves yourself is satisfying on so many levels. And doing it in a Dutch oven takes the experience to a whole new level.

The thick cast iron walls of a Dutch oven create the ideal enclosed environment for baking artisan style loaves. The tight seal traps steam in the initial baking stage which gives that delicious crackly crust. Since cast iron holds heat so evenly, you get perfect golden-brown crusts and moist interiors every time.

In this cookbook you'll learn all the tips and tricks for making incredible bread in your Dutch oven. We'll cover how to proof dough, shape loaves, score, and get that sought after oven spring. You'll find foolproof recipes for everyday loaves like Whole Wheat, Rustic French, and Sourdough. I'll share my top tips for troubleshooting any issues with your bakes.

Beyond basic breads, you'll find recipes utilizing the unique capabilities of the Dutch oven. Bake up beautiful braided Challah, sandwich-worthy Ciabatta, or showstopping loaves like Banana Bread, Pumpkin Spice, or Focaccia. The Dutch oven is also perfect for gentle overnight fermentation, so I've included no-knead and slow rise recipes too.

Preheat your ovens and grease up those Dutch ovens. This is going to be so much fun! Nothing smells better than a freshly baked loaf of bread. Let's get baking - I can't wait for you to enjoy these satisfying homemade loaves.

ALL ABOUT DUTCH OVEN BREAD BAKING

Baking bread in a Dutch oven is an excellent way to make homemade bread loaves. The Dutch oven traps steam and evenly distributes heat to produce bread with a crispy, glossy crust and an airy, pillowy interior. This guide covers everything you need to know about using a Dutch oven for bread baking.

What is a Dutch Oven?

A Dutch oven is a heavy, lidded cooking pot made of cast iron, ceramic, or enameled cast iron. Dutch ovens have been used for centuries to slowly cook stews, soups, and breads. The thick material retains heat well and distributes it evenly, creating ideal conditions for baking crusty bread.

Advantages of Dutch Ovens in Bread Baking

The Dutch oven provides an ideal environment for bread to rise, resulting in a light, airy interior and a crisp, glossy crust. Its ability to distribute heat evenly enhances the overall baking process, ensuring that every part of the bread, including the deep center, is perfectly baked. The trapped moisture in the form of steam keeps the crust soft for an extended period, allowing the dough ample time to rise. The outcome is bread with a glossy surface, impressive height, and a delightful airy texture.

Key Features for the Best Dutch Ovens for Bread

Discover the optimal Dutch oven materials, size, and shapes for baking delectable bread at home.

Material:
- **Cast Iron:** Opt for cast-iron Dutch ovens for their ability to withstand high baking temperatures and excellent heat retention and distribution, making them the preferred choice for bread baking.
- **Enameled Cast Iron:** While a matter of personal preference, enameled interiors are chosen by some bakers to prevent blackening and sticking. Ensure the enamel can endure the recipe's high temperatures.

Size & Shape:
- **5–7 Quart Capacity:** Choose a Dutch oven size that accommodates your dough amount to avoid dense interiors or flat loaves.
- **Oval Shape:** While round Dutch ovens work, the oval shape produces the classic bakery bread appearance.

Baking Tips & Tricks for Dutch Oven Bread

For fool-proof crusty Dutch oven bread, follow these guidelines:

- **Make Your Dough:** Use your favorite bread recipe and allow sufficient time for dough rising.
- **Fix Blackening:** Prevent burning by placing parchment paper in the Dutch oven. Use high-temperature-resistant paper.
- **Increase Steam:** Spritz water on the dough before baking for added steam.
- **Get Creative:** Experiment with ingredients like cheese, garlic, and herbs for a personalized touch.

Care and Maintenance of Dutch Ovens

Whether pre-seasoned or unseasoned, Dutch ovens require proper care:

Before First Use:
- Wash with hot sudsy water, avoiding abrasive cleaners.
- Coat with vegetable or food-grade mineral oil.
- Bake at 300°F–350°F for 30–60 minutes. Repeat oil coating and baking 5 or 6 times.

Cleaning and Storing:
- Clean promptly after each use with warm water and a scraper.
- Avoid soap; dry the oven thoroughly on medium heat.
- Apply a thin coat of vegetable oil inside before storing in a cool, dry place.
- Protect against moisture during storage with crumpled newspaper or a paper towel.

DUTCH OVEN SIZES AND CAPACITIES TABLE

Oven Size	Oven Capacity
5 inches	1 Pint
8 inches	2 Quarts
10 inches	4 Quarts
12 inches	6 Quarts
12 inches "Deep"	8 Quarts
14 inches	8 Quarts
14 inches "Deep"	10 Quarts
16 inches	12 Quarts

DRY MEASURE TABLE

Cups	Fl. Oz.	Tbsp.	Tsp.	ML.
1	8	16	48	237
¾	6	12	36	177
2/3	5 1/3	10 2/3	32	158
½	4	8	24	118
1/3	2 2/3	5 1/3	16	79
¼	2	4	12	59
1/8	1	2	6	30
1/16	½	1	3	15
1/48	1/8	1/3	1	5

LIQUID MEASURE TABLE

Gal.	Qt.	Pt.	Cups	Fl. Oz.	L.	Tbsp.	Tsp.
1	4	8	16	128	3.8		
½	2	4	8	64	1.89		
¼	1	2	4	32	.95		
	½	1	2	16	.47		
	¼	½	1	8	.24		
			½	4	.12	8	24
			¼	2	.06	4	12
			1/8	1	.03	2	6
				½	.015	1	3

KITCHEN MEASUREMENT ABBREVIATIONS (STANDARD AND METRIC) TABLE

Abbreviation	Measurement
Tbsp, tbsp, T.	Tablespoon
Tsp, tsp, t.	Teaspoon
Oz	Ounce
Fl. Oz	Fluid ounce
C.	Cup
Qt.	Quart
Pt.	Pint
Gal.	Gallon
Lb.	Pound
mL.	Milliliter
g.	Grams
Kg.	Kilogram
L, l	Liter

BASIC BREADS

1. Artisan Bread

Prep Time: 2 Hours 15 Minutes / Cook Time: 45 Minutes / Additional Time: 2 days / Total Time: Minutes / Yield: 20-24 slices

Ingredients:
- 1 teaspoon active dry yeast
- 3 cups all-purpose flour
- 2 teaspoons salt
- 1 ⅔ cups of warm water (110 degrees F or 45 degrees C)
- 1 teaspoon chopped fresh rosemary (Optional)
- 1 teaspoon chopped fresh thyme (Optional)
- 1 teaspoon chopped fresh sage (Optional)

Instructions:
1. Put the salt, yeast, and flour in a large bowl and mix them together. Mix in the water and herbs, if using. The dough will look shaggy and be extremely sticky. Warp the bowl with plastic wrap and leave it at room temperature for 18 to 24 hours.
2. Flour the work surface generously. After rising, the dough will be covered in bubbles. Place the dough on the work surface and sprinkle flour on top of it. Fold the dough in half, then shape it into a ball by stretching and tucking the dough's edges underneath the ball.
3. Flour a kitchen towel liberally (do not use terrycloth). Put the ball of dough on the floured towel. Cover again with another floured towel. Allow the dough to rise for around 2 hours.
4. Next, turn the oven on to 450 degrees F (230 degrees C). To preheat, put a Dutch oven (with a lid) inside the oven.
5. Take the baking dish out of the oven very carefully. Take off the cover and carefully place the dough ball, seam-side up, in the ungreased baking dish. Shake the dish to ensure that the dough is distributed more evenly.
6. Put a lid on it and bake for 30 minutes. Take off the lid and bake for 15-20 minutes or until the crust is golden brown. Take the loaf out of the pan and set it on a rack to cool. Then, cut it into pieces.

2. Beer Bread

Prep Time: 10 Minutes / Cook Time: 55 Minutes / Additional Time: 3 Hours / Total Time: 4 Hours 5 Minutes / Yield: 12 slices

Ingredients:
- ½ tablespoon instant yeast
- 1 ½ teaspoon salt
- 3 ¼ cup all-purpose flour
- 350 ml beer (your choice), room temperature

Instructions:
1. Mix the flour, yeast, beer, and salt in a large bowl or the stand mixer's bowl.
2. Now, mix on low speed with the dough hook until the dough starts to form and there is no more dry flour (about 2 minutes). If necessary, scrape down the bowl.
3. After the dough is formed, use your mixer to knead it for about five minutes, or until it becomes elastic and smooth.
4. Put plastic wrap or a damp kitchen towel over the bowl and allow it to rise for an hour and a half to two hours or until it doubles in size.
5. Dust a Dutch oven with a little flour and line it with parchment paper.
6. Pull the dough's edges into the middle to make a ball. Place it in the middle of the Dutch oven. Allow it to rest for an hour or until the size doubles.
7. Place the oven rack in the middle. Make a cross on top of the loaf by slicing two ¼-inch pieces with a sharp knife or razor. Do not preheat your oven.
8. Put the Dutch oven in the oven and cover it with its lid. Raise the oven to 400°F and cook the loaf for around 25 minutes.
9. Remove the lid carefully after 25 minutes and bake for an additional 30 minutes or until the top of the loaf is a deep golden brown.
10. Take the bread out of the Dutch oven and put it on a wire rack.
11. Allow it to cool completely before serving.

3. Ciabatta Bread

Prep Time: 10 Minutes / Cook Time: 20 Minutes / Additional Time: 4 Hours / Total Time: 4 Hours and 30 Minutes / Yield: 20-24 slices

Ingredients:
- 1 1/2 tsp. salt
- 4 cups flour (I do half wheat)
- 1/4 tsp. yeast
- 2 cups of hot water

Instructions:
1. Mix everything together, cover, and set aside for 8 to 18 hours or longer.
2. If you want to make the dough the same day, add an extra teaspoon of yeast and let it rise for at least four hours or until it looks like it's bubbling. It has a milder flavor but is still delicious.
3. When you are ready to bake, flour a cutting board (we use an IKEA one that is flexible) and put the dough on it, pressing it into a rough ball.
4. Put a Dutch oven inside and preheat the oven to 500 degrees (or 450 degrees, depending on how hot it is). When the dough ball is hot, cover it in the Dutch oven. Cook for around 20 minutes, then uncover and continue cooking until the tops are golden brown.
5. Take it out, let it cool, cut it up, and enjoy! Add some garlic, rosemary, and cracked pepper if you want a great savory bread.

4. Crusty No-Knead Bread

Prep Time: 10 Minutes / Cook Time: 40 Minutes / Additional Time: 3 Hours / Total Time: 3 Hours 50 Minutes / Yield: 20-24 slices

Ingredients:
- 2 tsp. instant yeast
- 2 tsp of salt or use 1½ tsp if you want less salt
- 2 cups hot water, about 125° F (54°C)
- 4 cups bread flour

Instructions:
1. In a big bowl, add the flour and create a well in the middle. Stir in the salt, yeast, and warm water until the flour absorbs all of the water.
2. After placing a tight-fitting lid or piece of cling wrap over the bowl, let it rest for two hours.
3. After 2 hours, uncover the dough and push it down to remove any trapped air. After that, roll the dough into a tight ball and put it on a big sheet of parchment paper.
4. Put a wet towel over it and let it rest for another hour.
5. In the meantime, turn on the oven to 450°F and put the Dutch pot inside for 30 minutes.
6. After one hour, remove the Dutch pot from the oven and carefully place the dough inside.
7. After covering it immediately, put it back in the oven and bake it for 30 minutes with the cover on and 10 minutes without.
8. Let it cool down for a while before you serve it. Enjoy!

5. Garlic Bread

Prep Time: 10 Minutes / Cook Time: 20 Minutes / Total Time: 30 Minutes / Yield: 20-24 slices

Ingredients:
- ½ cup parsley or other herbs
- pinch red pepper flakes
- ½ cup olive oil
- 5–10 cloves garlic
- 1 loaf of crusty artisan bread
- 1 cup shredded cheese
- ½ teaspoon salt

Instructions:
1. Slice the bread: To make squares, cut 1/2 to 1-inch slices both horizontally and vertically. Be careful not to cut through the bread completely, as you want the pieces to stay attached to the loaf's base. Put the loaf in the Dutch oven.
2. Make The Topps: Mince the parsley and garlic and combine with the salt, olive oil, and red pepper flakes.
3. Stuff The Bread: Drizzle the garlic-herb mixture, followed by the cheese, into the cracks with a spoon.
4. Cook for 10 to 20 minutes: Place the Dutch oven lid on top of 5 prepared coals. Put 15 coals on top of the lid. Bake until the bread is thoroughly warmed and the cheese is melted. (If making this at home, just bake it for 10-20 minutes at 350 degrees instead of camping.)
5. Serve And enjoy!

6. Honey Oat Bread

Prep Time: 30 Minutes / Cook Time: 40-45 Minutes / Total Time: 70-75 Minutes / Yield: 10-12 slices

Ingredients:
- 1½ teaspoons (4.5 grams) active dry yeast
- 1 teaspoon (3 grams) sea salt
- 2 tablespoons (37.5 grams) honey
- 1 cup of (100 grams) old fashioned rolled oats plus 2 tablespoons (12.5 grams) more to coat
- 2 cups (470 grams) water, room temperature
- 3¾ cups (487.5 grams) bread flour, plus more for dusting

Instructions:
1. First, Mix the yeast, water, and honey in a small bowl or use a measuring cup, then set aside until the yeast begins to foam, around 10-15 minutes. As the yeast starts to activate, combine the flour, oats, and salt in a big mixing bowl and set it aside.
2. In the bowl, put the yeast mixture and stir just until incorporated. The dough should be a little sticky and stringy, with a little flour around the edges of the bowl.
3. Now, cover it and allow it to rise in a warm place until it doubles in size.
4. When you're ready to bake, insert a covered baking dish or Dutch oven into the oven and preheat to 450°F (232°C). Your dough should be puffy and have risen to almost level (or higher) with the top of the bowl at this point. It will be hydrated and sticky.
5. Grease your shaping surface and hands (or a dough scraper, if using) with flour while the oven preheats. Pull the dough away from the bowl's edges and place it on the floured surface. Gently fold the dough into itself several times, adding flour if necessary to keep it from sticking, just until a soft ball covered in flour forms. After transferring the dough to parchment paper, evenly distribute the remaining oats over the top and sides, pressing them slightly into the dough. Allow to sit until the oven is preheated (20 minutes).
6. After preheating the oven, score your loaf and take the Dutch oven out of the oven. Next, place the dough, still on the parchment, in the Dutch oven. Bake with a cover on for 30 minutes, then take it off and continue baking for an additional 15-20 minutes. When the top of your bread begins to brown, it is done.
7. Using the parchment edges, remove the bread from the Dutch oven and place it on a wire cooling rack to cool for up to an hour before slicing.

7. Monkey Bread

Prep Time: 5 Minutes / Cook Time: 15 Minutes / Total Time: 20 Minutes / Yield: 6 slices

Ingredients:
- 1/4 cup brown sugar
- 4 tablespoons of butter (1/2 stick butter)
- 1 (16 oz) tube refrigerator biscuits
- 1/4 cup white sugar
- 2 tablespoons cinnamon
- 1/2 cup chopped walnuts
- Powdered sugar glaze optional for drizzled topping (combine powdered sugar with a bit of milk and vanilla extract to make a simple drizzle)

Instructions:
1. Heat the Dutch oven to 350 degrees Fahrenheit (17 coals on top of the lid and eight coals below the bottom of the oven).
2. Mix the brown sugar, cinnamon, nuts, and white sugar in a plastic bag.
3. Tear each biscuit into small pieces. Drop the biscuit pieces into the bag. Tightly seal the bag to prevent a big mess. Shake well to coat.
4. In the Dutch oven, melt the butter.
5. Next, transfer entire the contents of the bag into the oven, mix in the butter, and then cover the bottom with an even layer.
6. Bake, covered, for 15 to 25 minutes at 350 degrees Fahrenheit or until the dough is cooked. Placement of the coals: Make sure the bottom coals are set up in a circle so there is no "center coal." If there is a center of coal, the bread pieces in the middle will catch fire.
7. To ensure even baking, rotate the oven's bottom and lid in opposite directions every five minutes.
8. Take it off the heat and let it cool a bit before serving it hot.
9. If desired, drizzle powdered sugar glaze over the top.

8. No-Knead Cinnamon and Raisin Bread

Prep Time: 15 Minutes / Cook Time: 35 Minutes / Additional Time: 3 Hours / Total Time: 3 Hours 50 Minutes / Yield: 8 slices

Ingredients:
- 1 tablespoon bread flour
- 1 tablespoon white sugar
- 1 ½ teaspoons ground cinnamon
- ¾ cup golden raisins
- parchment paper
- ½ teaspoon dry instant yeast
- 1 ½ cups of warm water (110 degrees F or 43 degrees C)
- 1 teaspoon table salt
- 3 cups bread flour

Instructions:
1. Mix 3 cups of flour, sugar, cinnamon, salt, and yeast in a big bowl. Add water and stir until all of the flour is mixed in, and a wet, shaggy dough is formed. Include raisins and wrap in plastic wrap.
2. Now, place the bowl in a warm, draft-free area for 30 minutes, or place it in the oven with the oven light turned on.
3. Put 1 tablespoon of flour on a clean work surface. Spread the dough on the counter and use a bench scraper to fold it over several times. This will add most of the flour to the dough. Clean the bowl and pat it dry.
4. Trim the parchment paper into a bowl liner and fold it in half to rest flat against the bowl. Next, warp the bowl with plastic wrap and put the dough on the parchment paper. Allow to rise for 30 minutes.
5. Meanwhile, put a 5-quart Dutch oven inside and preheat it to 400 degrees Fahrenheit (or use 200 degrees C). Set the timer for 30 minutes.
6. Remove the warmed Dutch oven from the oven and place the dough in it, lined with parchment paper. Put a lid on top.
7. Bake for around thirty minutes in a preheated oven. Uncover and bake for another 5 minutes. Take the bread out of the oven and carefully place it on a wire rack. Take off the parchment paper. Let it cool for about two hours before cutting it.

9. No-Knead Whole Wheat Bread

Prep Time: 5 Minutes / Cook Time: 50 Minutes / Total Time: 55 Minutes / Yield: 12 slices

Ingredients:
- 3 ¾ cups of whole wheat flour or 480 grams
- 1 teaspoon dry active yeast
- 2 cups warm water between 100-115 degrees Fahrenheit
- 2 teaspoons of salt

Instructions:
1. Put the yeast, flour, and salt in a large bowl and mix them together. Use the wooden spoon or spatula to slowly add the water.
2. After covering the mixing bowl with plastic wrap or a fresh kitchen towel, leave it out at room temperature for at least eight hours or overnight.
3. After the dough has risen, put it on a lightly floured surface and shape it into a circle with a floured hand. While the oven heats up, let the dough rest.
4. Put a Dutch oven pan with a lid in the oven. Heat the oven to 450°F while the pan is in the oven.
5. When the oven is ready, carefully take the pan out of the oven and drop the shaped bread into the hot pan.
6. Bake the bread, covered, for 30 minutes. Take off the lid carefully, and bake for another 20 minutes.
7. Take the bread out of the Dutch oven and set it on the wire rack to cool for 10 to 15 minutes.

10. Oatmeal Bread

Prep Time: 15 Minutes / Cook Time: 45 Minutes / Total Time: 3 Hours / Yield: 20-24 slices

Ingredients:
- 100 g rolled oats (old-fashioned oats)
- 400 g bread flour
- 1 ½ salt
- 1 teaspoon dry active yeast
- 325 ml warm filter water

Instructions:
1. Put the flour, rolled oats, and warm water in a stand mixer with a dough hook.
2. Knead on low speed for around 5 minutes, cover, and allow dough to rest for around 1 hour. (To keep air from moving, I like to put the bowl in an oven that has been lightly heated.)
3. After this, put the salt on one side and the dry yeast on the other.
4. Take 15 minutes to knead. Put the lid on the bowl and let the dough rise for one hour and thirty minutes.
5. To release the gas and form the dough into a ball, gently crush the dough. Put parchment paper in a Dutch oven and put the dough on it.
6. Let the dough rise at room temperature for another 30 minutes.
7. Use a razor blade or use a sharp knife to cut the dough.
8. Place the Dutch oven inside the cold oven and cover it with the lid. To preheat, turn the oven's temperature up to 450°F. Depending on your oven, this process may take 40 to 45 minutes.
9. Bread should be carefully removed from the pot because it is extremely hot, and then allowed to cool completely before slicing.

11. Rustic French Bread

Prep Time: 3 Hours 30 Minutes / Cook Time: 50 Minutes / Total Time: 4 Hours 20 Minutes / Yield: 20-24 slices

Ingredients:
- 1 ¼ cups water 105 - 115 degrees
- 1 teaspoon salt
- 3 ¼ cups all-purpose flour
- 1 ½ teaspoon active dry yeast
- 1 teaspoon sugar

Instructions:
1. In the stand mixer bowl, mix sugar, yeast, and warm water. Allow for 5 minutes for yeast activation.
2. To the yeast mix, add half of the flour and salt. Attach the dough hook to the mixer and knead on medium-low speed. After adding the remaining flour, knead the dough just until it comes together. At this point, the dough will be sticky.
3. Move the dough to a lightly floured bowl and cover with a clean towel. Allow the dough to rise for around 2 hours. Move dough to a generously floured piece of parchment paper or cutting board and gently shape into a smooth ball. Put more flour on top of the dough, then put a big bowl over it and let it rise for another 30 minutes.
4. Warm the oven up to 425 degrees. Before baking bread, put the Dutch oven with the lid in the oven for 20 minutes to heat up.
5. Use a very sharp knife to make cuts on the top of the bread. Move the dough to the hot Dutch oven using parchment paper (or by itself if not using parchment paper). Put the lid on the pan and bake the bread for 30 minutes. Carefully take off the lid and bake for another 20 minutes, or until the top is golden.
6. Take the bread out of the oven and carefully move it to a rack to cool. Cut and serve after it has cooled! Bread can be kept on the counter for up to 3-5 days in a storage bag or container.

12. Soda Bread

Prep Time: 5 Minutes / Cook Time: 45 Minutes / Total Time: 50 Minutes / Yield: 12 slices

Ingredients:
- 1 1/2 tsp salt
- 1 ¾ cups buttermilk (14 oz)
- 1 T unsalted butter
- 4 cups of all-purpose flour, plus more for sprinkling (16 oz)
- 1 tsp baking soda

Instructions:
1. Warm the oven up to 425° F. To keep the bread from sticking, coat a Dutch oven with butter and then sprinkle with flour.
2. In the big bowl, mix the baking soda, flour, and salt. Next, add the buttermilk and stir to make a sticky dough. Gather the dough together and knead it gently for one minute. Then, roll it out into a thick disk shape. (about the size of your Dutch oven).
3. Place the dough flat on the center rack of the Dutch oven, cover, and bake for 30 minutes. Uncover and bake for 14 minutes more, or until the bread is golden brown and sounds hollow when tapped.
4. To keep the bread from drying out, put a clean towel over it and sprinkle it with a little water. Fresh is best, but it will keep at room temperature for up to 3 days. To keep the crusty texture, serve bread toasted with butter and jam.

13. White Bread

Prep Time: 10 Minutes / Cook Time: 45 Minutes / Additional Time: 12 Hours / Total Time: 12 Hours 55 Minutes / Yield: 8 slices

Ingredients:
- 1 tsp. salt
- 1 ½ cups warm water
- 3 cups white bread flour
- ½ tsp. Yeast rapid rise

Instructions:
1. Put the ingredients in a bowl, cover it, and let it rise for two hours.
2. Put the dough on a floured surface and roll it into a ball.
3. Now, cover the bowl and let the dough rest for 30 minutes.
4. Warm the oven up to 450 degrees.
5. Cover the Dutch oven and bake the dough for 30 minutes.
6. Uncover and bake for another 10-15 minutes.
7. Optional: Serve with jam.

14. Whole Wheat Bread

Prep Time: 20 Minutes / Cook Time: 40 Minutes / Additional Time: 8 Hours 45 Minutes / Total Time: 9 Hours 45 Minutes / Yield: 10 slices

Ingredients:
- ✓ 3 cups whole wheat flour
- ✓ 1 ½ cups warm water
- ✓ ½ teaspoon salt
- ✓ 1 teaspoon agave nectar
- ✓ 1 teaspoon active dry yeast

Instructions:
1. Fill water into a microwave-safe measuring cup and heat in the microwave oven for around 1 minute. Use a food thermometer to make sure the water isn't hotter than 100 degrees F (38 degrees C). Put in the agave and yeast. Wait about 15 minutes until the mixture foams up.
2. In the large bowl, mix the flour and salt together. Stir in the yeast mixture and knead a few times to combine. Cover the bowl and set it aside in a warm place to rise until doubled in size, about overnight to 18 hours.
3. Turn the dough out onto a floured surface. Knead the dough five to ten times with floured hands. Roll the dough into a ball and place it in the preheated oven to rise.
4. Put a Dutch oven inside the oven to warm for 30 minutes at 450 degrees Fahrenheit (230 degrees C).
5. Drop the dough into the hot Dutch oven using floured hands. Put the lid on the Dutch oven using potholders.
6. Bake for around 30 minutes in the heated oven. Open the Dutch oven and bake for another 10–15 minutes or until the bread is a deep golden-brown color. Take it off and let it cool.

15. Yeast Bread

Prep Time: 5 Minutes / Cook Time: 40 Minutes / Additional Time: 2 Hours / Total Time: 2 Hours 45 Minutes / Yield: 10-12 slices

Ingredients:
- ✓ 1 1/2 cups of (375 ml) very warm tap water, Not boiling or super-hot (55 °C/130°F)
- ✓ 2 tsp. cooking or kosher salt
- ✓ 3 cups (450g) flour, bread, or plain or all-purpose
- ✓ 2 tsp. Instant or rapid-rise yeast (normal or active dry yeast)

Dough shaping:
- ✓ 1 1/2 tbsp flour, for dusting

Instructions:
1. Make dough: In a big bowl, mix the flour, yeast, and salt together. After adding the water, mix the flour with the wooden spoon handle until it's all mixed in. The dough will be wet and sloppy, not kneadable, and not runny like cake batter. If you need to, add more water or flour to get the right consistency.
2. Rise: Cover with cling wrap or a plate and leave on the counter for 2–3 hours, or until it has doubled in volume. It is wobbly like jelly, and the top is bubbly. Move it somewhere warmer if it doesn't appear to be rising after an hour.
3. Optional: Put it in the fridge to let the flavors develop. You can either bake it right away or put it in the refrigerator for up to three days.
4. Remove the chill from the refrigerated dough. Place the bowl on the counter and let it sit for 45 to 60 minutes while the oven preheats. When the dough is cold, it doesn't rise as well.
5. Warm up the oven. Set the Dutch oven in the oven with the lid on (at least 26 cm/10"). 30 minutes before baking, heat the oven to 230°C or 450°F (220° fan).
6. Shape the dough: Put 1 tablespoon of flour on the work surface and remove the dough from the bowl. Add 1/2 tablespoon of flour on top.
7. Fold the sides inwards (about 6 folds) to form a roundish shape with a dough scraper or something similar (cake server, large knife, spatula). Don't be too careful because you're about to deform it. The goal is to deflate the dough bubbles and make a shape that you can move.
8. Transfer to paper: Place a large piece of baking paper or parchment (not wax paper) next to the dough, and turn the dough over so that the smooth side is up and the seam is down on the paper. Slide or push it to the center, then reshape it into a round shape. Don't worry too much about your shape. Actually, unevenness equals more ridges and crunchy bits!
9. The dough in the pot: Take the hot Dutch oven out of the oven. Put the dough into the pot on paper, then cover it with the lid.
10. Bake for 30 minutes with the lid on and then for 12 minutes without the lid on or until very golden and crispy.
11. Let it cool on the rack for 10 minutes before cutting it.

SPICES AND HERB BREAD

16. Cheddar-Dill Bread

Prep Time: 15 Minutes / Cook Time: 30 Minutes / Total Time: 2 Hours / Yield: 20-24 slices

Ingredients:
- 1 1/4 cups shredded cheddar, divided
- 1 package active dry yeast
- 1 tsp. salt
- 4 cups flour, divided
- 1 1/2 cups water
- 1 tbsp. dried dill
- 1 tbsp. sugar

Instructions:
1. Heat the water to a temperature of 105 to 115. Put yeast on top of the water and let it sit for 5 to 10 minutes.
2. In the meantime, mix salt, 3 cups of flour, and sugar in the bowl of a stand mixer or something similar. Add the yeast mixture and mix it in until everything is well mixed.
3. Put in a cup of shredded cheddar and some dried dill. Slowly stir in the remaining flour cup. The dough will stay sticky.
4. Use cooking spray in a medium Dutch oven. Put some flour on your hands and take the dough out of the mixer. Just add enough flour to make a ball, and then put it in the Dutch oven that has been prepared. Allow to rise for around an hour in a warm place, covered with plastic wrap, or until doubled in size.
5. Now, warm the oven up to 450 degrees F. Take off the plastic wrap, depress the dough, and shape it into a ball once more. Place it in the middle of the Dutch oven. Add the remaining 1/4 cup of shredded cheddar on top.
6. Bake for 30 minutes, uncovered, or until browned.
7. Take it out of the oven and let it cool in the Dutch oven. Take it out, cut it up, and serve immediately. Enjoy!

17. Cinnamon Raisin Bread

Prep Time: 3 Hours / Cook Time: 40 Minutes / Total Time: 3 Hours 40 Minutes / Yield: 10 slices

Ingredients:
- 1 1/2 tsp. active dry yeast
- 2 tsp. cinnamon
- 1/2 tsp salt
- 3 Tbsp. brown sugar
- 3 cups (360 grams) all-purpose flour
- 2/3 cup raisins
- 1 1/2 cups warm water

Instructions:
1. Prepare the dough: Put warm water, sugar, and yeast into an electric mixer. Stir and allow the yeast to activate for five minutes. I include sugar in this process because it feeds the yeast. Put in the salt, cinnamon, flour, and raisins. Using the bread mixing attachment, mix the ingredients together until a dough forms. If the dough is too wet or dry, add 1 tablespoon of water or flour at a time until the desired consistency is reached.
2. Let it rise: Toss the dough on a lightly floured surface and place it in a lightly greased bowl. Place a damp dish towel over it and leave it in a warm place for at least three hours. Double the size of the dough. (I like to put my dough in the oven with the light on (the oven is turned off).). This helps to maintain a consistent climate for the dough, while the light provides a small amount of warmth to help it rise.
3. Warm the oven up to 450F.
4. Move the dough: Put the dough on a lightly floured surface and roll it into a ball again. Keep flouring your hands to keep them from sticking. Place the dough on parchment paper. Lightly dust the paper to keep it from sticking. Lift the paper's edges to move the dough to the Dutch oven.
5. Bake: Put the lid on top and bake for 30 minutes. Then, take the lid off and bake for 5 to 10 more minutes, until the bread is golden brown.
6. Allow it to cool: After taking the bread out, let it cool for 20 minutes before cutting it.

18. Garlic and Herb

Prep Time: 5 Minutes / Cook Time: 40 Minutes / Additional Time: 1 Hour / Total Time: 1 Hour 45 Minutes / Yield: 8 slices

Ingredients:
- 1 packet Active Dry Yeast
- 3 cloves garlic, minced
- 1½ teaspoons ground Sea Salt Grinder
- 3 cups Baker's Corner All-Purpose Flour, plus additional for dusting
- 1½ cups hot water
- 1 tablespoon chopped rosemary
- 1/2 teaspoon Garlic Powder
- Pinch of ground Peppercorn Grinder
- 1 tablespoon chopped thyme

Instructions:
1. Preheat the oven to 450°.
2. Put flour, yeast, salt, pepper, herbs, garlic powder, and fresh garlic in a large bowl. Use a stir to mix.
3. Pour water into the bowl and mix it in. After covering it with plastic wrap, give it an hour to rise.
4. In the meantime, preheat the Crofton Cast Iron 6-Quart Dutch Oven in the oven.
5. After the dough has risen for an hour, put it on a floured surface, knead it 12 times, and then roll it into a ball. Place on a sheet of parchment paper and set aside.
6. Take the Crofton Cast Iron 6 Qt. Dutch Oven out of the oven and carefully put the dough and parchment paper inside. Put a lid on it and bake for around 30 minutes. Take off the lid and bake for another 10 minutes.

19. Italian Herbs and Cheese No-Knead Bread

Prep Time: 10 Minutes / Cook Time: 50 Minutes / Additional Time: 13 Hours / Total Time: 14 Hours / Yield: 20-24 slices

Ingredients:
- 2 teaspoons Kosher salt
- 1 cup of shaved Asiago cheese (or parmesan cheese)
- 1 teaspoon active dry yeast
- 1 ½ cups lukewarm water
- 3 cups all-purpose flour
- 1 tablespoon Italian seasoning
- optional: olive oil spray, flaky sea salt

Instructions:
1. Make the dough for the Italian bread with cheese and herbs: Make the dough about 12 hours before you want to bake the Italian herb Asiago cheese no-knead bread. Put the flour, Italian seasoning, Kosher salt, and active dry yeast in the large bowl and mix them together. Mix with a whisk. Stir in the Asiago after adding it. Slowly add the lukewarm water while stirring the dough with a wooden spoon until it is just combined. At this point, the dough will look rough and be very sticky, which is fine! Place a kitchen towel over the bowl and leave it in a warm, dry location for 12 hours.
2. Preheat the oven to 450°F for around 30 minutes before baking the bread. Make sure one of the oven's racks is in the center, and place an oven-safe Dutch oven (at least 4-quart) on the rack, lid on, to heat the oven while it preheats. Once the oven is preheated, leave the Dutch oven in the hot oven for another 20 minutes to ensure it's fully heated. I literally set a cooking timer for around 20 minutes once the oven is preheated.
3. To make the dough: Meanwhile, while the oven heats up, place the Italian herbs and cheese bread dough on a big piece of parchment paper. Using nonstick cooking spray on my hands makes it so much easier to work with the dough without it sticking.
4. Make the bread: When the Dutch oven is hot, carefully remove it from the oven. Take off the Dutch oven's lid quickly and carefully. Then, put the dough inside (you can just drop the parchment paper right in!). Cover the Dutch oven again, and put it back in the oven. Let it bake for 30 minutes. Take the Dutch oven out of the oven after 30 minutes. Take off the lid and spray a lot of olive oil spray on top of the Italian herb asiago cheese no-knead bread. If you want, you can sprinkle some flaky sea salt on top. Place the Dutch oven back in the oven and cook, uncovered, for around 20 minutes or until the loaf is golden brown and crusty.
5. Serve: Remove the bread from the Dutch oven carefully; you can just lift the parchment paper out of the Dutch oven. Before slicing or tearing the bread, let it cool slightly. Enjoy!

20. No-Knead Garlic Herb Bread

Prep Time: 15 Minutes / Cook Time: 40 Minutes / Additional Time: 12-18 Hours / Total Time: 13 Hours 10 Minutes / Yield: 20-24 slices

Ingredients:
- 1 1/2 cups lukewarm water
- 1/2 teaspoon active yeast
- 2 tablespoons dried Italian herb blend
- 3 cups all-purpose flour
- 2 teaspoons salt
- 5 cloves garlic, minced
- Flaky Salt (optional)

Instructions:
1. Whisk the yeast, salt, herbs, garlic, and flour together in a large bowl.
2. Stir in water gradually until a shaggy dough forms.
3. Now, cover the bowl with greased plastic wrap and set aside for 12-18 hours.
4. Warm the oven up to 450 degrees F when the dough is ready.
5. Put a 4-quart Dutch oven (with oven-proof lid) in the oven for 30 minutes.
6. While the dough is heating, place it on a piece of parchment paper large enough to line your Dutch oven.
7. Mix the flour into your hands and roll the dough into a ball. Put flaky sea salt on the top of the ball.
8. While the Dutch oven heats, cover with greased plastic wrap and set aside.
9. The hot Dutch oven should be carefully taken out of the oven, the dough-filled parchment paper placed inside, and the lid replaced.
10. Put it back in the oven and bake for around 30 minutes. Then, take off the lid and bake for 10 more minutes.
11. Move the bread and parchment paper to a baking rack and let them cool for a few minutes. Then, cut them into slices.

21. No-Knead Rosemary Parmesan Bread

Prep Time: 15 Minutes / Cook Time: 40 Minutes / Additional Time: 3 Hours 30 Minutes / Total Time: 4 Hours 15 Minutes / Yield: 20-24 slices

Ingredients:
- 1½ teaspoon salt
- 3 cups of all-purpose flour, plus another 2+ TB for working the dough
- ½ tablespoon dried rosemary, make sure it's chopped
- ¾ cup parmesan
- 2 teaspoons garlic powder
- sprinkle fresh, cracked black pepper
- 1½ cups hot water (115°-130°)
- ½ teaspoon quick-rise yeast

Instructions:
1. First, combine all dry ingredients in the large mixing bowls, leaving out the water and parmesan. Then add the hot water and mix again. I used a spoon made of wood.
2. Place it in a warm kitchen area and cover it with a damp towel or use plastic wrap. Let it sit for three hours. Move to another area of your home if your kitchen is particularly cold.
3. Sprinkle flour on a clean surface, then scrape the dough onto it. Use your hands or a spatula to flatten it out, then sprinkle ½ cup of parmesan on top and press it down. Shape the dough back into a ball by folding it around the edges and folding it for another four or so times.
4. Put the parchment paper back in the bowl and then add the dough. Add the rest of the parmesan on top, and if you have more, sprinkle more rosemary on top.
5. Put a lid on top and let it rise for another 30 minutes while you heat your oven to 450°F and place the Dutch oven inside.
6. After carefully taking the pot out of the oven, place the dough and parchment paper inside. Bake for 25-30 minutes with the lid on.
7. After removing the lid, bake the parmesan for an additional 5 to 8 minutes or until it turns golden.
8. Take the pot carefully out of the oven. Then, take the bread out of the pot and put it on a rack to cool for at least an hour before cutting it.

22. Olive Oil & Italian Herb Bread

Prep Time: 10 Minutes / Cook Time: 45 Minutes / Total Time: 55 Minutes / Yield: 10 slices

Ingredients:
- ½ cups Olive Oil Plus 2 Teaspoons
- ½ teaspoons Active Dry Yeast
- 1 cup Warm Water
- 3 Tablespoons Sugar
- 3 cups of All-purpose Flour, Plus More for Dusting
- 2 teaspoons Salt
- 2 teaspoons Cornmeal
- 1 teaspoon Italian Seasoning Blend

Instructions:
1. Mix the yeast, sugar, salt, Italian seasoning, and flour in a large bowl with a whisk. Mix in the 1/2 cup of olive oil and warm water with the wooden spoon or spatula until all the flour is mixed in and a soft dough form. Place the bowl on the counter for at least eight to ten hours (or overnight), covered with plastic wrap.
2. When the dough has risen and is bubbly and puffed, preheat the oven to 450°F. Once the oven is hot, put a Dutch oven pot in it without covering it for 30 to 40 minutes. In the meantime, place the dough on a lightly floured surface after removing it from the bowl with your hands coated in flour. Form the dough into a round ball with your hands. Set it aside while the Dutch oven heats up to 450°F.
3. After the Dutch oven has been at 450°F for 30 to 40 minutes, take it out of the oven. Add one teaspoon of olive oil to the pan's bottom and then sprinkle with one teaspoon of cornmeal. Put the dough ball carefully in the Dutch oven and use a sharp knife to make three or four cuts on top of it. Put the lid on the Dutch oven and drizzle the dough with the last teaspoon of olive oil. Then, sprinkle it with the last teaspoon of cornmeal.
4. Put it back in the oven and bake at 450°F for 30 to 35 minutes with the lid on. After around 30-35 minutes, remove the lid from the Dutch oven and bake for around 10 minutes or until the bread is golden brown. Take the pot out of the oven. Take the bread out of the Dutch oven and allow it to cool fully before enjoying it!

23. Rosemary Bread

Prep Time: 20 Minutes / Cook Time: 50 Minutes / Additional Time: 12 Hours / Total Time: Minutes 13 Hours 10 / Yield: 20-24 slices

Ingredients:
- 1½ cups water 341 grams, room temperature
- ¾ cup fresh rosemary leaves 22 grams, chopped
- ½ teaspoon active dry yeast 2 grams
- 3 cups all-purpose flour 360 grams
- 1¾ teaspoons sea salt 9 grams

Instructions:
1. Put the yeast, sea salt, rosemary, and flour in a large bowl and mix them all together. Add the water and blend with a spatula until everything is well-mixed.
2. Put the bowl on the counter for at least 12 hours and cover it with plastic wrap or a clean, damp dish towel.
3. With a Dutch oven inside, preheat the oven to 450°F.
4. After preheating, carefully take the Dutch oven out of the oven and take off the lid. Put on oven mitts!
5. Flour a clean work surface and your hands. After taking it out of the bowl, make a ball out of the dough. It's a no-knead recipe, but you might need to fold it a few times to get it to the right shape. Put the dough in the Dutch oven's bottom. (Be careful. Don't burn your hands; the cast iron will get hot!)
6. Put the lid on and bake for 30 minutes. Then take it off and bake for another 15-20 minutes until the bread is golden brown.
7. Take it out of the oven and let it cool down. Cut up and serve!

24. Rosemary Parmesan Bread

Prep Time: 20 Minutes / Cook Time: 40 Minutes / Additional Time: 2 Hours 10 Total Time: 3 Hours 10 Minutes / Yield: 20-24 slices

Ingredients:
- 1 tablespoon olive oil + more for brushing
- 1 1/8 cup shredded Parmesan cheese, divided
- 12 ounces (1 1/2 cups) water, 110-115 degrees
- 1 teaspoon active dry yeast
- 20-ounces bread flour, about 4 cups
- 1/4 teaspoon coarse sea salt
- 2 teaspoons kosher salt
- 1 1/2 tablespoons chopped fresh rosemary + more for topping

Instructions:
1. If you have a kitchen scale, put the mixing bowl on top to reset it. First, add 20 ounces of flour. Then, add the rosemary, olive oil, salt, and one cup of shredded Parmesan cheese. Put the scale back to zero and add 12 ounces of warm water. It should be 110 to 115 degrees Fahrenheit in the water. If you have one, you should use a kitchen thermometer to find out how hot it is. If not, check it with your finger. It ought to feel like a nice, warm bath. Add the yeast on top. If you don't have a kitchen scale, add the ingredients to the bowl by volume. Start with the bread flour, then add the rosemary, olive oil, salt, and finally the water. Add the yeast on top.
2. After the yeast dissolves, attach the paddle attachment to the mixer and mix on medium speed until the dough starts to come together.
3. Now, swap the attachment from the paddle to the dough hook. Mix on medium speed for ten minutes or until the dough is smooth and stretchy.
4. Place the mixing bowl in a warm place and cover it with the damp kitchen towel or use plastic wrap. Let it rise for around an hour or until it has doubled in size.
5. Move the dough to a lightly floured surface and knead it a few times to get rid of any extra air. Cover the dough and let it rest for around 10 minutes.
6. Make a boule out of the dough and put it in a Dutch oven that has been greased with olive oil or lined with parchment paper. Cover it again and let it rise for another hour.
7. Warm the oven up to 450 degrees.
8. Once the dough has risen, score or slice an X on top and brush it with olive oil. Sprinkle coarse sea salt on top. Put the lid on top and bake for 30 minutes.
9. After taking it out of the oven, brush it with olive oil and sprinkle it with fresh rosemary and 1/8 cup of Parmesan cheese. Bake it uncovered for another 10 minutes or until the top is golden brown.
10. Take it out of the oven and let it rest for around 10 minutes before cutting it up and serving it.

25. Rosemary Thyme No-Knead Bread

Prep Time: 10 Minutes / Cook Time: 45 Minutes / Additional Time: 12 Hours / Total Time: 12 Hours 55 Minutes / Yield: 4 slices

Ingredients:
- 1 1/2 tsp salt
- 1/4 cup olive oil
- 1 1/2 tbsp fresh thyme chopped
- 1 1/2 tbsp of fresh rosemary finely chopped
- 3 cups all-purpose flour
- 1/2 tsp instant yeast
- 1 1/4 cups room temperature water

Instructions:
1. Mix the yeast, salt, rosemary, and thyme with the flour in a large bowl. Mix the water and olive oil into the dough with a wooden spoon until the flour is fully mixed in. The dough will be sticky and wet.
2. Place the bowl in a warm kitchen area and leave it there for ten to eighteen hours, covered with plastic wrap. The dough will be puffed and double in size.
3. Sprinkle flour on a clean work surface, and dump the dough out of the bowl. You can use your hands or a wooden spoon to help you get it all out. A few folds over will make the dough a little more stable. Sort of gently stretch the top of the dough and pull the ends under the loaf to make a ball.
4. Now, spray a piece of parchment paper with olive oil. After placing your dough on the parchment, cover it with a paper towel or damp kitchen towel. Put it somewhere warm in the kitchen and let it rise for another hour to an hour and a half.
5. Preheat the oven to 500 degrees Fahrenheit for 30 minutes before you plan to bake your bread in a large Dutch oven with a lid or (other heavy, lidded, oven-safe pot). Ensure you can heat the pot and lid up to 500 degrees.
6. Once the Dutch oven is warm, take it out of the oven. This is where I set off the fire alarm, but it was okay. Attach the dough loaf to the corners of the parchment paper and gradually lower it into your Dutch oven, paper, and all. Put the lid on top and put it back in the oven.
7. Then, turn down the heat to 425 degrees and cook for 30 minutes with the lid on.
8. Take off the lid and bake for 15 more minutes. Set the loaf down on a wire rack to cool.
9. Cut one or more slits in the top of the bread dough with a serrated knife before you bake it.

26. Rustic Herb Loaf

Prep Time: 2 Hours / Cook Time: 1 Hour / Total Time: 3 Hours / Yield: 12 slices

Ingredients:
- 2 1/4 teaspoons of active dry yeast (1 envelope)
- 2 teaspoons of coarse salt, plus more for sprinkling
- 1/2 cup unsalted butter (113 grams)
- 1 heaping tablespoon fresh herbs, chopped (used rosemary, thyme, and sage)
- 1 cup warm water (250 ml)
- Olive oil
- 3–4 cups bread flour (567 grams)

Instructions:
1. First, add yeast to warm water and let it sit for 5 minutes.
2. In a small saucepan, melt the butter. Take it off the heat and add the fresh herbs. Allow it to cool a bit.
3. Mix salt and 2 cups of bread flour in the bowl of a stand mixer with a dough hook. After adding the yeast and butter, mix the dough until it comes together. Put the remaining flour, a quarter cup at a time, until the dough fills the bowl and feels slightly sticky to the touch.
4. Use the electric mixer with a dough hook and knead until the dough is nicely smooth and elastic, about 5 minutes. You can knead it by hand, too, but it will take longer.
5. After covering, wait about an hour for the rise to double.
6. Warm the oven up to 450 degrees F. Put parchment paper inside a cast iron Dutch oven or grease it with olive oil.
7. Punch the dough down and knead it by hand a few times. Reshape and put in the prepared Dutch oven. Cut a pretty deep "x" into the dough with a sharp knife. Put some olive oil on top, then coarse salt and more herbs.
8. Put a lid on it and let it rise for another 30 minutes.
9. Put the Dutch oven lid on and bake for 30 minutes. Take off the lid and bake the loaf for another 15 to 30 minutes until it is golden brown. Allow to cool completely before cutting.

27. Sun-Dried Tomato Basil No Knead Bread

Prep Time: 15 Minutes / Cook Time: 1 Hours / Additional Time: 12 Hours / Total Time: 14 Hours 45 Minutes / Yield: 20-24 slices

Ingredients:
- 1 tsp Sutter Buttes Tuscan Herb Sea Salt
- 1 cup water
- ½ tsp instant yeast
- 3 cups all-purpose flour
- ½ cup of sun-dried tomatoes in oil, drained and chopped
- ¼ cup Sutter Buttes Tomato Basil Dipping Sauce, plus additional for serving

Instructions:
1. First, Mix the yeast, salt, and flour in a bowl. Add water, olive oil, and sun-dried tomatoes and mix well. It will be a very sticky dough. Put plastic wrap over the bowl and let it rise for at least 12 hours.
2. Set a piece of parchment paper aside after the dough has risen. Take out the dough from the bowl, put it on a floured surface, and then gently form it into a round loaf.
3. Place the bread on the baking sheet. Put a damp towel over it and let it sit for at least an hour.
4. Warm the oven up to 450 degrees. After covering it, put the Dutch oven in the oven and cook for half an hour.
5. Take the Dutch oven out of the oven after 30 minutes.
6. Now, use the parchment paper to lift the bread and carefully put it into the Dutch oven base. (To keep it from sticking, the parchment paper is placed inside the Dutch oven).
7. Put the lid on the Dutch oven and put it back in the oven. Set the oven to 300°F.
8. Take off the lid and bake the bread for another 30 minutes until it starts to turn brown.
9. Let the bread cool on a rack, then cut it up and enjoy!

28. Tomato and Olive Focaccia

Prep Time: 20 Minutes / Cook Time: 35-40 Minutes / Additional Time: 1-2 Hours / Total Time: 2 Hours 30 Minutes / Yield: 8-10 slices

Ingredients:

- 1/2 teaspoon Himalayan Sea salt ground
- 1 tablespoon Cornmeal to dust Dutch oven
- 2 tablespoons extra-virgin olive oil + 1 teaspoon for greasing
- 1/2 teaspoon sugar
- 4 cups All-Purpose Flour
- 1 cup warm water more if needed
- 1 envelope Active Dry Yeast 2 teaspoons

Topping:

- Italian Herbs
- Campari tomatoes, whole or sliced
- Grated Parmesan cheese
- Himalayan Sea Salt coarse (pink salt)
- Black Olives, pitted
- Fresh Basil for garnish

Instructions:

1. Put 4 cups of all-purpose flour and salt in a large bowl. Make a well after mixing.
2. Add sugar and dry yeast to a bowl. Add one cup of Luke-warm water, stir, and wait a minute or two. Slowly mix the flour with the sugar water and activated yeast. Use the wooden spoon to mix everything together, and then begin kneading.
3. Knead the dough for ten minutes or until it forms a ball and isn't as sticky as it was before.
4. Put the olive oil on top. Place it on top of a clean kitchen towel and cover it with plastic foil (film or plastic wrap). This will keep it warm. Allow it to rise for about one or two hours or until it has doubled in size.
5. Preheat the oven to 425°F (220°C) and heat a Dutch oven with a lid for about 2 minutes. Carefully take it out of the oven.
6. Then, put olive oil on the Dutch oven and its sides, and then add the cornmeal.
7. Knead the dough for a few minutes, then place it in the Dutch oven. Stretch as far as possible to cover the entire bottom. Use a fork or something similar to poke holes in the dough. Then, sprinkle it with coarse pink salt and herbs.
8. Arrange whole Campari tomatoes and pitted black olives wherever you'd like. Let the dough rise for three to four minutes. Cover the Dutch oven and move it to a preheated oven.
9. Set the oven to 400F and bake for 20 minutes. After 20 minutes, completely remove all the Campari tomatoes from the wine. Because it's going to be hot, please be careful. Bake the focaccia for an additional 10 to 15 minutes, removing the lid. The crust should be golden. In the last five minutes, put those tomatoes on top of the wine.
10. Wait at least 10 minutes before cutting it. Add more herbs and Parmesan cheese, and serve with fresh basil. Serve the "roasted" Campari tomatoes with a drizzle of olive oil on the side, or place them back on the focaccia.

GRAIN, SEED, AND NUTS BREADS

29. Cranberry Walnut Bread

Prep Time: 5 Minutes / Cook Time: 50 Minutes / Additional Time: 12 Hours / Total Time: 12 Hours 55 Minutes / Yield: 16 slices

Ingredients:

- 1 ½ teaspoons salt
- 3 cups of white wheat flour or unbleached all-purpose flour
- ½ cup dried cranberries
- ½ chopped walnuts
- 1 ½ cups lukewarm water
- 1 teaspoon dry active yeast

Instructions:

1. Put the flour, yeast, salt, cranberries, and walnuts in a large bowl and mix them together. Use a wooden spoon to mix the water well.
2. Place in a draft-free area and cover with plastic wrap or a clean kitchen towel. Let rise for 12 to 18 hours without being touched.
3. After the proofing time has passed, quickly shape the dough into a circle on parchment paper that has been lightly dusted with flour. You might want to flour your hands, too, because it will be sticky. Also, try not to work the dough too much; you only need a rough circle. While the oven heats up, let the dough rest.
4. Put the Dutch oven in the oven with its lid on top. Warm up to 450 degrees F. (Put the pan in the oven to heat up.)
5. Once the pan is hot, take it out of the oven carefully and carefully put the prepared dough in it. Then, put the lid on top of the pan and bake. Using parchment paper that is safe to use up to 450 degrees Fahrenheit, all you have to do is pick it up and slide it into the Dutch oven. If you don't have parchment paper, simply place the bread dough in the Dutch oven. Do not use silicone or wax paper for baking.
6. Cover and bake for 30 minutes. Take off the lid and bake for twenty more minutes.
7. Take the bread out of the Dutch oven and allow it to chill completely on a wire rack. Then, cut it into pieces and serve.

30. Cranberry, Chia Seed & Almond No Knead Bread

Prep Time: 10 Minutes / Cook Time: 45 Minutes / Additional Time: 18 Hours / Total Time: 18 Hours 55 Minutes / Yield: 10-12 slices

Ingredients:
- 1 tbs Chia Seeds
- 1/2 tsp Active Dry Yeast
- 3 Cups Flour
- 1.5 Cups Water Room Temperature
- 1/8 Cup Slivered Almonds
- 1/4 Cup Dried Cranberries

Instructions:
1. Using a spoon, combine all the dry ingredients (flour, cranberries, almonds, chia seeds, and yeast) in a medium-sized bowl.
2. Add the water at room temperature and mix it with a spoon.
3. Now, allow the bowl to sit at room temperature for 12 to 18 hours with the plastic wrap over it tight.
4. Let the dough rise for 12-18 hours. Then, put the Dutch oven with the lid on into a cool oven and heat it up to 450 degrees F. Before adding the dough, you want to make sure the Dutch oven reaches 450 degrees.
5. After the oven reaches 450 degrees, take out the Dutch oven and cover, then add the dough into the Dutch oven. Sprinkle some flour on the bottom of the Dutch oven to keep the bread from sticking, and keep adding flour to your hands as you shape the dough into a ball.
6. After baking for 30 minutes with the lid on, take it off and continue baking for a further 10 to 15 minutes or until the top is nicely browned.
7. Get the bread out of the Dutch oven and let it cool down before you serve it.

31. Mulitseed No-Knead Bread

Prep Time: 10 Minutes / Cook Time: 40 Minutes / Total Time: 50 Minutes / Yield: 20-24 slices

Ingredients:
- ½ cup (50g) oats
- 1 ½ cups (340g) of warm water
- 1 teaspoon salt
- 400 g bread flour and more for dusting
- 1 tablespoon sugar
- 2 ¼ teaspoon dry yeast
- ½ cup (80g) mixed seeds and 1 tablespoon extra for topping

Instructions:
1. Place the sugar, yeast, and finger-warm water in a mixing bowl. Allow it to sit for 10 minutes. Then, use a spoon to mix in the flour, salt, oats, and mixed seeds. It will be sticky and loose. Now, wrap it in plastic wrap and allow it to rise for around one hour.
2. After an hour, heat the oven to 230 C (450 F). Heat the Dutch oven with a lid in the oven for about 30 minutes.
3. Using a well-floured piece of parchment paper, scrape out the dough. Put some flour on your hands so the dough no longer sticks to them.
4. Pull the dough's edges toward the middle slowly to make a ball. Brush a little water on top of the bread as you turn it over. Put mixed seeds on top and cover with the kitchen towel until the Dutch oven is hot.
5. It will be very hot when you take the Dutch oven out.
6. Remove the lid and carefully lift the bread inside using the parchment paper. Bake for thirty minutes with the lid on. After that, take the lid off and bake for another 5 to 10 minutes.
7. Before slicing, allow the bread to chill for around thirty minutes. It is best when eaten freshly baked; it keeps well for two days. Slice and freeze the leftovers to enjoy later.

32. Multigrain Bread

Prep Time: 20 Minutes / Cook Time: 30 Minutes / Additional Time: 5-6 Hours / Total Time: 6-7 Hours / Yield: 20-24 slices

Ingredients:
- 2/3 cup (53 grams) old-fashioned oats
- 2 tablespoons (28 grams) brown sugar
- 1¼ cups of (128 grams) dark rye flour, plus more for dusting
- 1 cup of (130 grams) whole wheat flour
- 2 cups (254 grams) bread flour
- ¼ cup (36 grams) raw shelled sunflower seeds
- 1¾ cups of plus 2½ tablespoons (432 grams) warm water (105°F or 41°C to 110°F/43°C)
- 1 tablespoon (9 grams) black sesame seeds
- 1 tablespoon (9 grams) kosher salt
- 1 tablespoon (9 grams) flax seeds
- 1 teaspoon (2 grams) fennel seeds
- 2¼ teaspoons (7 grams) instant yeast

Multi-Seed Topping:
- 1 ½ teaspoons (4.5 grams) flax seeds
- 1 tablespoon of (5 grams) old-fashioned oats
- 2 teaspoons of (6 grams) raw shelled sunflower seeds
- 1 ½ teaspoons of (4.5 grams) black sesame seeds
- 1 teaspoon (3 grams) fennel seeds

Instructions:

1. Put the flour, oats, sunflower seeds, brown sugar, salt, sesame seeds, flax seeds, yeast, and fennel seeds in a large bowl. Mix in 1¾ cups plus 2½ tablespoons (432 grams) of warm water by hand until everything is mixed in and a sticky dough forms. The flour, oats, sunflower seeds, brown sugar, salt, sesame seeds, flax seeds, yeast, and fennel seeds can also be put in the bowl of a stand mixer with the paddle attachment. After adding 1¾ cups and 2½ tablespoons (432 grams) of warm water, beat on medium speed for around 30 seconds or until a sticky dough forms.
2. Cover and let rise for two hours in a warm (75°F/24°C) place with no drafts. After that, put it in the refrigerator for at least two hours, but preferably overnight.
3. Place the dough on a lightly floured surface and press it down just enough to make it level. Fold the dough's edges toward the center, pressing gently, starting on the left side and moving clockwise. Now, flip the ball of dough over a cup and pull it toward you with both hands. Repeat after flipping the dough 90 degrees until you have a round that is smooth, sealed, and taut.
4. Dust a piece of parchment paper with rye flour. Place the dough on the paper so the seam side faces up. Cover and let rise for around one hour in a warm (75°F/24°C) place with no drafts.
5. It's time for the dough to rise. Put the 6- to 7-quart Dutch oven and lid in a cold oven. Warm the oven up to 260°F (500°C).
6. Be careful when taking the hot Dutch oven out of the oven. Take off the lid and quickly place the bread inside the Dutch oven so that the seam is on the bottom. Brush the top of the loaf with water, then sprinkle with the Multi-Seed Topping. Score the top of the bread. Put the dish back in the oven and cover it with the lid.
7. Lower the oven's temperature right away to 450°F (230°C). Set the oven to 250°F. Take off the lid and bake for another 15 minutes or until an instant-read thermometer inserted in the middle reads 190°F (88°C). Take the loaf out of the Dutch oven immediately and place it on a wire rack to chill completely.
8. In a small bowl, stir Multi-Seed Topping all ingredients. Finally, Serve with topping.

33. No Knead Bread with Seeds

Prep Time: 10 Minutes / Cook Time: 35 Minutes / Total Time: 45 Minutes / Yield: 20-24 slices

Ingredients:

- ✓ 2 ¼ tsp or use 1 packet rapid rising yeast
- ✓ 1 tbsp flax seeds
- ✓ 1 tbsp sunflower seeds
- ✓ 1 tbsp chia seeds
- ✓ 1 ½ cups + 2 tbsp warm water 95 – 105 degrees F
- ✓ 1 ½ tbsp pumpkin seeds
- ✓ 3 cups bread flour OR all-purpose flour
- ✓ + an extra sprinkle of all the seeds
- ✓ 2 tbsp almond slices
- ✓ 1 tsp salt
- ✓ 3 tbsp sugar

Instructions:

1. Mix the flour and seeds together in a big bowl, then create a well in the middle.
2. Mix warm water, sugar, yeast, and salt in a medium-sized bowl. Mix with a whisk.
3. Fill the well in the big bowl with the water-yeast mix.
4. Use a wooden spoon to mix it until it starts to form a dough.
5. Put the dough on a floured surface and work it together for three minutes or until there are no more flour streaks. If it's too sticky, add more flour. If it's too dry, add more water. The dough will be soft and slightly bumpy to slightly smooth.
6. Roll the dough into a rough circle and put it in a bowl that has been lightly greased. Cover with a tea towel or other gentle cloth and plastic wrap. Now, allow the dough to double in size at room temperature, around 1 ½ - 2 hours, in a warm spot.
7. Warm the oven up to 450F.
8. Take the dough out of the bowl and lay it out on a counter dusted with flour. Fold four corners into the middle with a light press to make a ball. Remove it from the bowl and put it, seam-side down, on a piece of parchment paper, exposing the smooth side. Use your hands to make the dough ball a little more round. Add more seeds and brush with water.
9. Cut the loaf down the middle with a small, sharp paring knife. After the oven has reached temperature, place the Dutch oven inside for 15 to 20 minutes.
10. Next, take the Dutch oven out of the oven and remove the lid.
11. Lift the parchment paper's edges to put the dough into the Dutch oven carefully. Close the lid again.
12. After 30 minutes of baking, take off the lid and continue baking for around 5 minutes, or until the cake is nicely golden!

34. No Knead Fruit and Nut Bread

Prep Time: 5 Minutes / Cook Time: 40 Minutes / Additional Time: 18 Hours / Total Time: 18 Hours 45 Minutes / Yield: 10 slices

Ingredients:
- ¾ Tsp instant yeast
- ½ Cup dried cranberries
- 2 Tsp salt
- 3 Cups all-purpose flour (420 g)
- ½ Cup pecans
- 1½ TO 1¾ CUPS water
- ½ Cup walnuts
- 1 Cup whole wheat flour (140 g)
- ½ Cup golden raisins

Instructions:
1. Mix the yeast, salt, and flour in the large bowl. Put the nuts and dried fruit and stir to mix. Make sure all the ingredients are well mixed. Add the water and combine everything. The dough should be shaggy and sticky. Simply mix and flip the dough until all dry ingredients are gone.
2. Now, allow the dough to rest at room temperature for 12 to 18 hours while the bowl is covered. It gets more flavorful as you let it sit for longer. The dough will have risen and might be slightly darker after 18 hours than when you first started.
3. Put a piece of parchment paper on the counter and sprinkle a lot of flour over it. Using wet hands, fold the dough over on itself several times to let out the air inside. Roll the dough into a ball and place it, seam side down, on the floured parchment paper.
4. Sprinkle a little more flour over the dough, then flip the mixing bowl over to cover the dough. (Alternatively, you could cover the dough with a clean kitchen towel, but I find that this sticks to the dough a lot and ruins the towel's appearance as well as the bread's.)
5. Allow the dough to rest like this for up to 2 hours. Once the dough has rested on the counter for one to one and a half hours, insert a cast iron Dutch oven with a lid into your oven and preheat it for thirty minutes to 425°F.
6. Next, carefully take the Dutch oven out of the oven and remove the lid. Use a baker's lame or a serrated knife to cut three slashes in the top of the bread. Apply the parchment paper to lift the shaped dough into the pot. Place the lid on top of the dough and the paper on top of it. Put the pot back in the oven and wait 30 minutes.
7. After 30 minutes, take off the Dutch oven's lid and continue baking the bread for a further 10 to 15 minutes or until the top is nicely browned. Take the pot out of the oven and let the bread rest for five minutes. After that, move the lovely loaf to a rack to cool. It will be hard not to eat the bread right away, but wait 30 minutes before you do.

35. No Knead Quinoa Bread

Prep Time: 15 Minutes / Cook Time: 45 Minutes / Additional Time: 3-4 Hours / Total Time: 4-5 Hours / Yield: 20-24 slices

Ingredients:
- 1 1/2 Tbsp instant yeast
- 3 Cups white whole wheat flour
- 3 1/4 Cup water
- 1 T kosher salt
- 1/4 Cup vital wheat gluten
- 3 1/2 Cups unbleached all-purpose flour
- 1 Cup whole quinoa

Instructions:
1. First, Mix the dry ingredients with a whisk in a large bowl or dough-rising bucket (at least 5 quarts).
2. Mix in the water using a dough whisk, your hands, or a big wooden spoon.
3. Set the dough somewhere warm for two hours with the lid on top.
4. The dough can be kept in the fridge for up to 10 days or at least 24 hours.
5. When you're ready to bake, cut a 1-pound loaf (1/4 of the dough) into a ball on a floured work surface.
6. Put the dough onto a small piece of parchment paper, seam side down. Take the dough out of the bowl and into a soup bowl. Wrap it up in plastic wrap.
7. Allow to rise for about 90 minutes.
8. Now, heat the oven to 450 degrees F and put it in a Dutch oven.
9. When the dough is ready, take out the Dutch oven from the oven, uncover it, and place the dough, parchment, and all into the Dutch oven. Cut the dough, put it back in the oven, and cover it.
10. Bake for fifteen minutes, remove the lid, and continue baking for ten to twenty minutes. The internal temperature of the bread should be around 200°F.
11. Let cool on a wire rack.

36. Poppy Seed Bread

Prep Time: 15 Minutes / Cook Time: 45 Minutes / Additional Time: 30 Minutes / Total Time: 1 Hour 30 Minutes / Yield: 20-24 slices

Ingredients:
- 3 1/2 Tbs. oil
- 1/2 tsp. almond extract
- 1 tsp. baking powder
- 3/4 cup sugar
- 2 eggs
- 1/4 cup butter, melted
- 1/2 tsp. vanilla
- 3/4 tsp. poppy seeds
- 1/2 cup milk
- 1/2 tsp. salt
- 1 cup flour
- Orange Almond Icing:
- 1/4 tsp. vanilla
- 1/4 tsp. almond extract
- 1/4 cup powdered sugar
- 1 Tbs. orange juice

Instructions:
1. Mix butter, oil, eggs, milk, sugar, vanilla, and almond extract together in a bowl. Put the flour, salt, baking powder, and poppy seeds in a different bowl. Add to the first mix and mix it well, but only mix it a little.
2. Pour the mixture into your oiled Dutch oven and bake for around 45 minutes at 325°F (four hours if you're like me!). Serve plain or with icing made of orange almonds. Mix all the ingredients for the icing in a small bowl and drizzle it over the bread.

37. Pumpkin Seed Bread

Prep Time: 10 Minutes / Cook Time: 30 Minutes / Total Time: 40 Minutes / Yield: 20-24 slices

Ingredients:
- ½ tsp instant yeast
- 1 cup pumpkin seed
- 2 tsp salt
- 3 cups of Bob's Red Mill Artisan Bread flour
- 1½ cups + 2 Tbsp room temperature water

Instructions:
1. In a big bowl, mix together the flour, salt, yeast, and pumpkin seeds. Mix them together with a whisk.
2. Mix the flour and water together and stir until a thick dough forms. It will be slightly sticky and scrappy. Now, wrap the bowl in plastic wrap and rest overnight at room temperature.
3. Heat the oven to 450 degrees when you're ready to bake. To heat it up, put a big enamel Dutch oven (6 QT) in the oven for 30 minutes.
4. Put the dough out of the bowl on a clean, well-floured work surface. Next, roll the dough into a ball and sprinkle some flour on top of it. Cover with plastic wrap until the Dutch oven is hot.
5. Take the plastic off of the dough. Fill a piece of parchment paper large enough to line the Dutch oven with dough. Be careful when you put the dough on parchment paper in a hot pan.
6. Cover and bake for 30 minutes. Take it out of the oven when the top is golden brown and crispy.
7. Warm up and serve.

38. Raisin Walnut Bread

Prep Time: 15 Minutes / Cook Time: 1 Hours / Additional Time: 8-9 Hours / Total Time: 9-10 Hours / Yield: 20-24 slices

Ingredients:
- 1 cup chopped walnuts
- 2 teaspoons ground cinnamon
- 3 cups cool water (70° to 75°)
- 1 cup raisins
- 2 teaspoons salt
- 1/4 cup sugar
- 2 teaspoons active dry yeast
- 6-7 cups (125 grams per cup) all-purpose flour

Instructions:
1. Mix 6 cups of flour, sugar, yeast, cinnamon, and salt together in a large bowl. Add the walnuts and raisins and mix them in. Then add water and enough of the rest of the flour to make a soft, shaggy dough. Do not knead. Let it rise in a cool place for 7-8 hours with the lid on.
2. Warm the oven up to 450°. Put the Dutch oven with the lid in the middle of the rack and heat it for at least 30 minutes. Once the Dutch oven is hot, turn the dough out onto a well-floured surface. Make a round loaf quickly with a metal scraper or spatula. Put it on top of a piece of parchment paper carefully.
3. Cut a 1/4-inch-deep slash across the top of the loaf with a sharp knife. With the parchment, lower the loaf immediately into the hot Dutch oven. Bake for 30 minutes with the lid on. Take off the lid and bake the loaf for another 20 to 30 minutes, or until it is a deep golden-brown color and sounds hollow when tapped. If the bread begins to brown too quickly, cover it partially. Take the loaf out of the Dutch oven and let it chill fully on a wire rack.

39. Yogurt Flaxseed Bread

Prep Time: 20 Minutes / Cook Time: 40 Minutes / Total Time: 1 Hour / Yield: 20-24 slices

Ingredients:
- 1 cup (100 g) whole wheat flour
- 1 teaspoon clear honey
- 20 g fresh yeast (0.7 oz) or use 1 package of dried yeast (7 g or 0.25 oz)
- 2 teaspoons fine sea salt or Kosher
- ½ cup (150 g) low-fat yogurt
- 3 tablespoons flaxseed
- 2 ½ cups (300 g) all-purpose flour
- ¾ cup (175 ml) lukewarm water

Instructions:
1. Put together: In the stand mixer, combine the flour, salt, and flaxseed and mix for a few seconds. If you use instant yeast, you should also mix it with the flour.
2. If using active dry yeast, mix the honey and yeast in lukewarm water, then let stand for five minutes or as directed on the package.
3. Knead: Add to the mixer along with the yogurt and knead with the dough hook for around 3 minutes (or as long as your stand mixer's kneading instructions specify) or until the dough becomes elastic and less sticky.
4. Now, move the dough to a lightly floured work surface and knead it for a short time, just long enough to make it roughly round.
5. Rise up: After placing the dough in a bowl and lightly dusting it with flour, cover it with a new kitchen towel and let it rise until doubled in size, which should take approximately an hour, depending on your kitchen's temperature.
6. Second rise: Put the bread back on the work surface and knead it for a short time. Put a piece of parchment paper on the work surface and then put the dough ball on it. Cover with a towel again and set it on the counter to rise while preheating the oven.
7. Preheat: Put the Dutch oven and its lid in the oven. To begin, preheat the oven to 230 degrees Celsius, or 450 degrees Fahrenheit.
8. Move the dough: Carefully grab the sides of the parchment paper and drop the dough and paper into the hot Dutch oven. Put on mitts, because the dish is very hot! Put the lid on top of it and put it in the oven.
9. Put the lid on and bake for around 25 minutes. Take off the lid and bake for another 10-15 minutes or until the bread is golden brown.
10. Make sure: Take the bread out of the pot and tap it with your knuckles to ensure it's baked all the way through; it should sound hollow. Let it cool all the way down on a wire rack.

CHEESY BREADS

40. Artisan Ham & Cheese Bread

Prep Time: 15 Minutes / Cook Time: 45 Minutes / Total Time: 1 Hour / Yield: 20-24 slices

Ingredients:
- 3 teaspoons kosher salt
- cornmeal for pot
- 2 tsp yeast
- non-stick spray for pot
- 2 cups sharp cheddar cheese, grated
- 6 cups of all-purpose flour, (plus more for dusting)
- 2 cups fully cooked ham, diced
- 3 cups Luke-warm water

Instructions:
1. Mix the yeast, salt, and flour together in a large bowl.
2. Put the water and stir the mixture with a wooden spoon or a Danish whisk until it looks like shaggy dough.
3. Put a plastic lid or plastic wrap over the dough. Place the lid on top of the bowl but do not press down tightly. Allow it to sit at room temperature for 8 to 18 hours. The dough will rise and bubble.
4. Add the ham and cheese, mix well, and chill the dough.
5. Warm the oven up to 450° degrees when the dough is ready.
6. Put the dough on a well-floured surface and roll it into a ball with your floured hands. Pour into a stainless-steel bowl that has been lightly oiled. Allow the dough to rest while covered with a thin towel.
7. Now, spray the pan with nonstick spray and then sprinkle cornmeal on top.
8. Put your Dutch ovens in a hot oven for 30 minutes while the dough rests.
9. After 30 minutes, carefully take out the Dutch oven and transfer the bread dough to the heated pan.
10. Put the lid back on and bake for another 30 minutes. Then, take off the lid and bake for 15 minutes more without it.
11. It's best to let the bread cool for an hour before cutting it.
12. The bread will be golden, crusty, and tasty!

41. Cheddar Sage Bread

Prep Time: 20 Minutes / Cook Time: 30 Minutes / Additional Time: 5-6 Hours / Total Time: 6-7 Hours / Yield: 20-24 slices

Ingredients:
- 1 teaspoon (2 grams) rubbed sage
- 1¾ cups plus 2 tablespoons of (425 grams) warm water (105°F or 41°C to 110°F/43°C)
- 2¼ teaspoons (7 grams) instant yeast
- 1 tablespoon (9 grams) kosher salt
- 3 cups (381 grams) bread flour
- 1 cup (130 grams) whole wheat flour
- 1 (8-ounce) block (226 grams) extra-sharp aged white Cheddar cheese
- Corn flour for dusting

Instructions:
1. Put yeast, salt, bread flour, and whole wheat flour in a large bowl. Add 1¾ cups plus 2 tablespoons of warm water and mix it in with your hands until it's all mixed in and a sticky dough form. Alternatively, put the yeast, bread flour, whole wheat flour, and salt in the stand mixer bowl with a paddle attachment attached. Mix in 1¾ cups of warm water plus 2 tablespoons of it. Now, beat on medium speed for about 30 seconds or until a sticky dough forms.)
2. Cover and let rise for two hours in a warm (75°F/24°C) place with no drafts. After that, put it in the refrigerator for at least two hours, preferably overnight, or for up to five days. (The flavor will get stronger the longer the dough sits.)
3. Cut the cheddar block in half (113 grams each). Cut one half into 12-inch cubes and finely grate the other. Combine grated cheese and sage in a small bowl.
4. Place the dough on a lightly floured surface, sprinkle it with flour, and roll it out to a thickness of 1 inch. Spread about two-thirds of the cubed cheese and grated cheese-sage mixture onto the dough. Fold the dough's edges toward the center, pressing gently, starting on the left side and moving clockwise. Reroll the dough to a 1-inch thickness, sprinkle with the remaining cubed cheese and grated cheese-sage mixture, and fold it back to the center. Next, flip the ball of dough over a cup and pull it toward you with both hands. To create a tight, sealed round, turn the dough 90 degrees and repeat the process. It is fine if some of the cheese cubes poke through the dough.
5. Dust a sheet of parchment paper heavily with corn flour, then place the dough on it, seam side up. Cover and let rise for around one hour in a warm (75°F/24°C) place with no drafts.
6. When the dough has risen for 30 minutes, place a 6- to 7-quart Dutch oven and lid in a cold oven. Warm the oven up to 260°F (500°C).
7. Be careful when taking the hot Dutch oven out of the oven. Take off the lid and quickly place the bread inside the Dutch oven so that the seam is on the bottom. Score the top of the bread. Cover with a lid and return to the oven.
8. Immediately lower the oven's temperature to 230°C (450°F). Set the oven to 250°F. Take off the lid and bake for another 15 minutes or until an instant-read thermometer inserted in the middle reads 190°F (88°C). Take the loaf out of the Dutch oven immediately and place it on a wire rack to chill thoroughly.

42. Cheesy Herb Artisan Bread

Prep Time: 20 Minutes / Cook Time: 45 Minutes / Additional Time: 12 Hourr / Total Time: Minutes / Yield: 8-10 slices

Ingredients:
- ¼ tsp Garlic Salt
- 3 cups flour
- ½ tsp Marjoram
- 1 cup Grated Parmesan Cheese
- ½ tsp Thyme
- 1 tsp salt
- ½ tsp Basil
- ½ tsp Oregano
- 1 ½ tsp sugar
- 1 ½ tbsp Olive Oil
- 1 ½ cups warm water
- 1 ½ tsp instant yeast granules
- 2 tbsp melted butter

Instructions:
1. Mix the flour, salt, yeast, sugar, oregano, thyme, marjoram, and parmesan in a large bowl. Put the olive oil and warm water and mix them together. It will be a sticky dough.
2. Now, allow dough to rise in a covered bowl for 12 hours or until doubled in size.
3. Lightly flour a surface, then knead the dough four or five times.
4. Put parchment paper inside the Dutch oven. Cover the dough in a Dutch oven with a towel and set aside to double in size.
5. Warm the oven up to 450 degrees. Cover the Dutch oven and bake for around 30 minutes. Remove the lid, then use melted butter to brush and sprinkle garlic salt on top. Bake for 15 minutes more.
6. Remove, allow to cool for a few minutes, then slice and enjoy.

43. Cheesy Italian Bread

Prep Time: 5 Minutes / Cook Time: 45 Minutes / Additional Time: 8 Hours / Total Time: 8 Hours 45 Minutes / Yield: 8-10 slices

Ingredients:
- 4 cups flour, divided
- 1 3/4 teaspoon salt
- 3/4 teaspoon Italian seasoning, divided
- 1 1/2 cups of warm water
- 1/2 cup shredded mozzarella cheese
- 1/2 teaspoon active dry yeast

Instructions:
1. Put 3 cups of flour, salt, yeast, and warm water in a large bowl. Toss the ingredients together with a spatula until they are well mixed. Put it on the counter for at least 8 hours with a towel or plastic wrap over it.
2. Now, warm the oven up to 450 degrees F. Put the Dutch oven in the oven to warm up as well until the dough ball is finished.
3. After dusting a surface with flour, take the dough out of the bowl. Put on half a teaspoon of Italian seasoning and then the mozzarella. First, use your hands to mix it, and then add the extra cup of flour. Mix the flour into the dough by kneading it. Make a ball out of it.
4. After that, spread olive oil on the bottom of the Dutch oven pan and place the dough ball on top of it. On top of the ball, sprinkle the last 1/4 teaspoon of Italian seasoning.
5. Place the lid on top and bake for 30 minutes. After that, take the lid off and bake for another 15 minutes or until the bread is golden brown.

44. Cheesy Pull Apart Garlic Bread

Prep Time: 5 Minutes / Cook Time: 15 Minutes / Total Time: 20 Minutes / Yield: 4 slices

Ingredients:
- 3 large cloves of garlic
- 1 round Italian or sourdough bread loaf
- 1/2 cup unsalted butter
- 1/4 cup of fresh parsley or basil (chopped)
- 1/4 tsp. salt
- 6 oz. shredded mozzarella cheese

Instructions:
At Home:

1. First, bring the butter to room temperature and mash it with a fork when it's soft enough.
2. Cut up the garlic. For this, I use a fine grater.
3. Mix in the garlic and salt with the softened butter.
4. Wrap the butter in wax paper and put it in the cooler. I like to spread the butter thinly before wrapping it to allow it to come to room temperature faster at camp.

While at camp:

1. Remove the butter from the cooler and allow it to thaw enough to spread.
2. Using a chimney starter, begin heating your briquettes. You'll need about 22–25 briquettes.
3. Slice your bread horizontally, but do not cut all the way through to the bottom. The loaf should still be able to hold together.
4. Use a lot of the garlic butter you made at home to cover one side of each slice of bread.
5. Fill each slice with shredded cheese.
6. Finally, cut the bread into bite-sized squares by slicing it vertically, but only some of the way through.
7. Put parchment paper around the edges of your Dutch oven to make it easier to clean, then carefully put your cheese bread inside. Put the lid on top.
8. Preheat the Dutch oven to 425°F, using briquettes on both the top and bottom. Cook until the cheese is completely melted, around 15 minutes.
9. At last, take the Dutch oven off the heat and add chopped basil or parsley to the bread. Enjoy!

45. Jalapeno Cheddar

Prep Time: 10 Minutes / Cook Time: 50 Minutes / Additional Time: 2 Hours / Total Time: 3 Hours / Yield: 8 slices

Ingredients:
To A Medium Mixing Bowl:

- 1 large jalapeno, diced
- 2 cups shredded cheddar cheese
- 3 1/2 cups bread flour
- 1 1/2 tsp. kosher salt

To a large mixing bowl:

- 2 1/4 tsp. of instant yeast (1 standard .25oz packet)
- 2 cups warm water

For the topping:

- 10 round slices jalapeno (or more, to taste)
- 1/3–1/2 cup shredded cheddar

Instructions:
1. Put bread flour, salt, 2 cups of cheddar cheese, and diced jalapenos in a medium-sized bowl. Mix it up and set it aside.
2. Place the yeast and warm water in a large bowl. The water should be warm but not hot (like bath water for babies). Put the flour mixture into the yeast and water mixture. Use a rubber spatula to mix everything together until there are no more flour streaks.
3. Fold the dough in on itself 8–10 times with a spatula from the outside of the bowl towards the center, turning the bowl slightly each time.
4. To let it rise, cover it with a towel and put it in a warm place for an hour.
5. After an hour, fold the dough eight to ten times more with the rubber spatula. Put a towel over it and allow it to rise in a warm place for another hour.
6. Preheat the oven to 450°F and place your Dutch oven inside, lid on, halfway through the second rise. Allow it to heat up for 30 minutes. Prepare a piece of parchment paper big enough to fit inside your Dutch oven with some overhang.
7. Dust a counter or cutting board lightly with flour, and then flour your hands. Place the dough on the floured surface. Move the dough around and brush off any extra flour.
8. Make a rough ball by folding the dough's corners in towards the middle about 6 to 8 times. Turn the dough over onto the parchment paper.
9. Now, carefully score the dough with a sharp knife (I like to make an "X"). Spray a little cooking spray (or brush on some oil) on the dough, then sprinkle on the 1/3–1/2 cup of cheese that has been set aside and add the sliced jalapenos.
10. Remove the hot Dutch oven from your oven and take off the lid using oven mitts. Use the parchment paper to move the dough to the Dutch oven. Return to the oven and put the lid back on.
11. Put the lid on and bake for 30 minutes. Then, take it off and bake for another 20 minutes.
12. After that, remove the Dutch oven from the oven, tilt it slightly, and slide the bread and parchment out of the pot using the parchment. It'll be easy to get out.
13. Before slicing, remove the parchment paper and allow the bread to chill on the wire rack for one to two hours. The texture of the bread should be completely cool before it is sliced.

46. No Knead Cheddar Bread

Prep Time: 5 Minutes / Cook Time: 50 Minutes / Additional Time: 12 Hours / Total Time: 12 Hours / Yield: 8 slices

Ingredients:
- 1 1/2 cups water
- 1 1/4 cups of shredded sharp cheddar cheese
- 3 cups flour
- 2 teaspoons salt
- 1/2 teaspoon yeast

Instructions:
1. Mix the yeast, salt, and flour together in a large bowl using a whisk.
2. Mix in the water and keep mixing until a sticky dough forms.
3. Add the cheddar cheese and mix it into the dough until it's fully mixed in.
4. Cover the dough and let it sit for 12 to 18 hours at room temperature.
5. When you're ready to bake your dough, preheat the oven to 450 degrees Fahrenheit and place a Dutch oven inside.
6. While the oven is heating up, lightly flour a smooth surface and roll the dough into it until it forms a ball.
7. Once the oven is ready, take out the hot Dutch oven, line it with parchment paper if you want, and put the bread dough into the Dutch oven.
8. Put the lid on top of the Dutch oven and bake the bread for 30 minutes. Then take the lid off and cook for another 15 to 20 minutes, or until the bread is golden brown.
9. Take it out of the oven and let it cool down. Cut it up and enjoy!

47. No Knead Cheese Bread

Prep Time: 15 Minutes / Cook Time: 45 Minutes / Additional Time: 3-5 Hours / Total Time: 4-6 Hours / Yield: 8-10 slices

Ingredients:
- 3 cups all-purpose flour, plus 1/4 cup for dusting
- 1 tsp salt
- 1/2 teaspoon dry active yeast
- 1 1/2 cups warm water, 95F–105F
- 1 1/2 cups cheddar cheese
- 1 cup chives, thinly sliced
- 3 tbsp. fresh thyme

Instructions:
1. First, mix flour, salt, and yeast in a large bowl with a whisk. Add warm water and mix it in completely with your hands or a wooden spoon. The dough should stick together. Put plastic wrap over the bowl and let the dough rest for three to five hours. If you want the mixture to start to bubble on top, it should double in size. This can stay out on the counter for 18 hours.
2. When you're ready to bake, put a Dutch oven in a 450F oven that has been preheated. Allow 30–40 minutes for the Dutch oven to preheat. When the oven is heating, flour a flat surface and your hands before removing the dough from the bowl. Four times, fold the dough over itself. Put some cheese and herbs on top of each fold. After that, make a tight ball with your hands. After putting a piece of parchment paper into your bowl, carefully drop the ball of dough into it. Place a kitchen towel over it and let it sit for 20 minutes.
3. When your Dutch oven is very hot, carefully take it out, take off the lid, and put the dough ball and parchment paper into the Dutch oven. Cut a hole in the top of the dough with sharp knife to let the steam escape. Put the Dutch oven's lid back on, and bake for 30 minutes.
4. Take off the Dutch oven lid after 30 minutes and bake the bread for another 15 minutes, or until it is a beautiful golden brown color.
5. Take it out of the oven and let it cool for 10 minutes. Then cut it up and enjoy!

48. Rosemary Cheese Bread

Prep Time: 25 Minutes / Cook Time: 50 Minutes / Total Time: 1 Hours 15 Minutes / Yield: 10 slices

Ingredients:
- 3 ½ cups (455 g) bread flour
- 1 cup (132 g) Gruyere cheese, grated
- 1 tablespoon freshly chopped rosemary
- 12 ounces (354 ml) lukewarm water
- 1 ½ teaspoons salt
- ½ cup (80 g) cornmeal
- 2 ¼ teaspoons Active Dry Yeast, 1 packet
- ½ teaspoon ground black pepper

Instructions:
1. Put the flour, salt, pepper, yeast, ¾ cup of cheese, and rosemary in a large bowl. Use a whisk to mix. Add the water slowly. To make the dough into a ball, mix it with a wooden spoon until it is well mixed.
2. Put plastic wrap over the bowl and allow it on the counter overnight, for 8 to 24 hours.
3. Now, spread the dough out onto a lightly floured surface. Using well-floured hands, flatten the dough into a 9-inch circle, then roll it into a ball by folding it over and over. Transfer the dough into a smaller bowl than the Dutch oven you intend to bake it in, and lightly grease it. Place a tea towel over the bowl and allow it to rise for two hours or until it has doubled in size.
4. In the meantime, place a 4 to 6-quart Dutch oven on the oven rack that is positioned in the lower third of the oven. Warm the oven up to 450°F.
5. After the dough has risen, take the Dutch oven out of the oven and take off the cover. Put a lot of cornmeal on the bottom of the Dutch oven. Carefully put the dough inside, then sprinkle the rest of the cornmeal on top. Warp the Dutch oven with the lid and put it back in the oven.
6. Set the oven to 300°F. Take the lid off the Dutch oven and add the rest of the cheese. Bake for another 15 to 20 minutes without covering. Once the bread is cool, take it out of the Dutch oven and set it on a wire rack.

49. Smoky Pepper Bread

Prep Time: 15 Minutes / Cook Time: 40 Minutes / Total Time: 5 Hours / Yield: 8 slices

Ingredients:
- 1 (0.25-ounce) package instant yeast
- 1 3/4 cups plus 2 tablespoons of warm water (105°F/41°C–110°F/43°C)
- 1 1/4 cups 1/4-inch-cubed Monterey Jack cheese with peppers
- 1 teaspoon garlic powder
- 1/2 teaspoon ground black pepper
- 3 cups of bread flour, plus more for dusting
- 1 cup of whole wheat flour
- 1 tablespoon kosher salt
- 1 tablespoon smoked paprika

Instructions:
1. Mix bread flour, whole wheat flour, salt, paprika, yeast, garlic powder, and black pepper in a large bowl with a whisk. Add the cheese and stir it in until it is covered in the flour mixture. Stir in 1 3/4 cups plus 2 tablespoons of warm water until the water is fully mixed in and a sticky dough form. Cover and let it rise for two hours in a warm place with no drafts.
2. Put the dough in the refrigerator for at least two hours and up to one night.
3. Dust a work surface lightly with bread flour; place dough onto the prepared surface; gently press the dough to smooth and level. Starting on the left side of the dough and working your way around it clockwise, lightly push the edges of the dough towards the middle. Turn the dough ball over, cup it, and pull it towards you with both hands. Turn the dough 90 degrees and do it again until you have a round that is smooth, tight, and sealed.
4. After that, dust a piece of parchment paper with a lot of bread flour. Place the dough on the parchment, seam side down. Cover and set aside in a warm, draft-free place to rise for 1–12 hours or until puffed and the dough holds an indentation when gently pressed.
5. When the dough has about 30 minutes to rise, place a 6- to 7-quart Dutch oven with a lid in a cold oven. Warm the oven up to 260°F (500°C).
6. Score the top of the dough as desired with a lame or sharp knife. Trim the parchment to extend 2 to 3 inches around the sides of the dough.
7. Carefully take the hot Dutch oven out of the oven and take off the lid. Quickly put the dough inside the Dutch oven, using the parchment as handles. Put it in the oven and cover it with a lid.
8. Immediately lower the oven's temperature to 230°C (450°F). Bake for thirty minutes. Take off the lid and bake for another 10 minutes or until the instant-read thermometer inserted in the middle reads 190°F (88°C). Carefully take the loaf out of the Dutch oven right away and place it on a wire rack to cool completely. Keep it in a container that keeps air out for up to three days.

FRUIT BREADS

50. Apple Yeast Bread

Prep Time: 10 Minutes / Cook Time: 40 Minutes / Total Time: 14 Hours 50 Minutes / Yield: 10 slices

Ingredients:
- cornmeal
- 220 ml 100 F (38 C) warm water
- 7 g active dry yeast
- 25 g sugar
- 1-2 large red apples
- extra flour
- 480 ml (g) water
- 7 g active dry yeast
- 220 g all-purpose unbleached white flour
- 800 g all-purpose unbleached white flour
- 20 ml (g) milk
- 1 pinch salt

Instructions:
1. Use a thermometer to find out how warm the water is (220 ml), and add 7g of active dry yeast to a medium-sized bowl. Let it sit for 8–10 minutes until it starts to bubble. Later, add 220g of flour and use a spatula to mix it in. Let it rise at room temperature for 12 hours or overnight, covered with a clean kitchen towel.
2. Create the dough for the bread. Mix 800g of flour, 7g of yeast salt, sugar, 480 ml of water, and 20ml of milk. Knead the dough on low for at least 20 minutes or until it is sticky and stretchy.
3. Place the clean kitchen towel over the bowl where the dough was mixed, and let it rise at room temperature for 45 minutes.
4. Peel and core the apple, then cut it into small pieces and fold it into the bread dough gradually.
5. Now, place the dough in a bowl lined with parchment paper. Warp with the clean kitchen towel and let it rise again at room temperature for 45 minutes. OR (this is better!) Put a dish towel on the counter, sprinkle it with a lot of flour and cornmeal, and then put the dough on the towel. Cover it and let it rise.
6. Set the oven to 450F and put the Dutch oven with the lid inside for 15 minutes into the second rise. Heat the oven and Dutch oven for at least 30 minutes.
7. Next, carefully remove the Dutch oven from the oven, turn it over, and carefully tip the bread out of the bowl using the edges of the parchment paper.

Alternatively, take a dish towel and place the dough inside the blazing Dutch oven. Put the lid back on top and put it back in the oven. Bake for 30 minutes with the lid on and 10 more minutes without it.
8. Take the Dutch oven out of the oven, take the bread out of the Dutch oven, and put it on a cooling rack. Wait until the bread is completely chilled before cutting it into pieces.

51. Banana Bread

Prep Time: 15 Minutes / Cook Time: 30 Minutes / Additional Time: 10 Minutes / Total Time: 45 Minutes / Yield: 8 slices

Ingredients:
- 2 teaspoons cinnamon
- ½ cup softened butter
- 4 ripe bananas
- 1 ½ cups flour
- 1 egg, beaten
- 1 teaspoon baking soda
- Pinch of salt
- 1 cup brown sugar
- 1 tablespoon bourbon, optional

Instructions:
1. Combine the brown sugar, cinnamon, baking soda, and salt in a bowl using a whisk. Put away.
2. Make a bed of about 20 coals or a campfire.
3. With a fork, mash the bananas in the large bowl until they are pretty smooth. Stir in the bourbon, egg, and butter until everything is well-mixed.
4. Now, stir the dry mixture into the wet ingredients until it is fully combined.
5. Put a piece of parchment paper inside your Dutch oven. This will help keep the bread from getting stuck in the pot.
6. Place the batter in the Dutch oven and put the lid on top. Set the Dutch oven on top of a ring of five coals. Cover the lid with the remaining 15 coals.
7. Bake for around half an hour.
8. Take the pan off the heat and carefully take the bread out of the oven.
9. Let it cool down for a while, then cut it up and enjoy!

52. Blueberry Bread

Prep Time: 2 Hours / Cook Time: 40 Minutes / Additional Time: 20 Minutes / Total Time: 3 Hours / Yield: 16 slices

Ingredients:
- 1 packet of rapid-rise yeast
- 4 cups of all-purpose flour
- 2 cups of warm water
- A pinch of salt
- 1 cup of blueberries
- ¼ c softened unsalted butter
- 2 tablespoons of olive oil
- 1 tablespoon of lemon juice
- ½ cup light brown sugar, combined

Instructions:
1. Mix yeast and warm water in a medium-sized mixing bowl (around 110 degrees F is ideal when working with yeast). Stir gently to combine.
2. Let the yeast and water bloom for ten minutes or until the mixture starts to foam.
3. Put the flour and a pinch of salt to a second bowl. Stir.
4. In the flour mixture, make a well. Add ¼ cup of brown sugar to the flour mix.
5. When the yeast is ready, add it to the flour right away.
6. Mix the dough together with a spoon until it's all mixed together. The dough will be shaggy and extremely sticky.
7. Place the dough back in the bowl where the yeast has bloomed. Drizzle some olive oil on top of the dough and cover it.
8. After the dough has doubled in size, let it rest and rise. It takes an hour to do this.
9. Put the blueberries, ¼ cup of brown sugar, lemon juice, and softened butter in a small bowl.
10. Add the blueberries to the dough.
11. Lift the edges of the dough with a spoon and allow the blueberries to settle at the bottom of the bowl. Some of the berries should be pressed into the dough. Put a lid on top and let it rise for another 30 minutes.
12. Rub some olive oil or butter into the sides of the Dutch oven while the dough rises again.
13. Put the Dutch oven inside the oven and heat it up to 400 degrees.
14. With care, take the Dutch oven out of the oven after 30 minutes and put the bread dough inside. Be careful because it will be extremely hot!
15. Now, cover the Dutch oven and bake the bread for 30 minutes.
16. Remove the lid after 30 minutes. You can add a little butter on top if you'd like. Bake for an additional 10 minutes.
17. Be careful when you take the Dutch oven out of the oven, and let the bread rest in it for 10 minutes before you take it out.

53. Cherry Walnut Loaf

Prep Time: 15 Minutes / Cook Time: 2 Hours 15 Minutes / Total Time: 2 Hours 30 Minutes / Yield: 12 slices

Ingredients:
- ½ cup Organic Ground Flax Seed by Wild Oats
- 1 teaspoon Baking Soda
- ¼ cup Apple Cider Vinegar
- 6 large Raw Egg Whites
- ¾ cup Warm Water
- 1 ½ cups Almond Flour
- ½ cup Walnuts
- 2 large Whole Raw Eggs
- 1 tsp Coarse Kosher Salt by Morton
- ⅓ cup Dried Fruit Unsweetened Unsulfured Dark Sweet Cherries by Trader Joe's
- ½ cup Coconut Flour
- ¾ cup Original Coconut Milk Unsweetened by Silk
- ⅓ cup Fiber life Whole Ground Psyllium Husk

Instructions:
1. Warm the oven up to 450 F. As soon as the oven turns on, put a 6-quart Dutch oven inside with the lid on so that it can heat up together with the oven. Use the whisk to mix all the dry ingredients together in a bowl.
2. Put in the walnuts and dried cherries.
3. Add the wet ingredients (except the water) to the dry ingredients and combine them together using a whisk.
4. Pour ¼ cup of water at a time. Add the next ¼ cup at a time and mix until all the water is mixed in.
5. Make a round ball out of the loaf. With care, take the hot Dutch oven out of the oven, take off the lid, and spray nonstick cooking spray inside. Fill the Dutch oven with the rounded dough. After covering with the lid, bake it for 15 minutes.
6. Turn the oven down to 300 F and take off the lid. Bake for another two hours or until the food is fully cooked.
7. Let it cool down before cutting it.

54. Cranberry Orange Bread

Prep Time: 15 Minutes / Cook Time: 45 Minutes / Additional Time: 12-24 Hours / Total Time: 13-25 Hours / Yield: 8-10 slices

Ingredients:
- 1 ½ cup warm water
- zest of two oranges
- 3 cup flour
- 1 cup dried cranberries
- 1 tsp. yeast
- 1 t sp. salt

Instructions:
1. Mix the yeast, salt, cranberries, and zest in a large bowl with a whisk. Pour water and stir until a shaggy mixture forms. (You want the mixture to be loose and sticky). Place the bowl in a warm place for 12 hours or up to 24 hours with plastic wrap covering it. It works great overnight.
2. Turn the oven on to 450. Heat a cast iron Dutch oven with a lid in the oven for 30 minutes. Meanwhile, place the risen dough on a heavily floured surface (the mixture will be sticky) and shape it into a round loaf.
3. After taking the hot pot out of the oven, carefully add the dough. Return to the oven for another 30 minutes, covered. After that, take off the lid and bake for another 10 to 15 minutes. Carefully take the bread out of the oven and the pot and set it on a rack to cool.

55. No Knead Fruit Bread

Prep Time: 20 Minutes / Cook Time: 35 Minutes / Additional Time: 14 Hours / Total Time: 14 Hours 55 Minutes / Yield: 8 slices

Ingredients:
- 100 g raisins
- 400 g bread flour
- 1¼ teaspoon salt
- ½ teaspoon ground cinnamon
- ¼ teaspoon bake yeast
- 325 ml water
- 1 teaspoon ground mixed spice

Instructions:
1. First, in a large bowl, mix the dry ingredients together.
2. Using a fork, mix the hand-hot water with the dry ingredients until all of the ingredients are combined.
3. Cover and set aside for about an hour, then move to the refrigerator when it has slightly risen. Allow to rise for at least 12 hours or overnight. After that time, the dough should have risen.
4. Warm the oven up to 220C (425F). When the oven is nearly at that temperature, put the empty casserole dish with a lid in it to preheat.
5. Take the dough from the refrigerator for a few minutes before baking the loaf to allow it to warm slightly.
6. Put the dough on a lightly floured pastry board, fold it over itself several times, and shape it into a ball. Add a little more flour if the dough is too sticky.
7. Put the dough ball on a piece of baking parchment that doesn't stick.
8. After removing it from the oven, place the preheated dish on a heatproof surface.
9. Place the dough on top of the parchment paper in the preheated casserole dish. Cut a slit in the top of the dough with a sharp knife.
10. After covering the casserole dish, bake it in the oven's center for around 30 minutes. Keeping the lid on during baking will help release steam and enable the loaf to rise before the crust forms.
11. Take off the lid and put it back in the oven for another 5 minutes or until it's browned.
12. Take out of the casserole dish and set aside to cool on a wire rack. Enjoy your fruit bread without kneading now.

56. Cranberry Pistachio Bread

Prep Time: 15 Minutes / Cook Time: 50 Minutes / Additional Time: 10-12 Hours / Total Time: 11-12 Hours / Yield: 20-24 slices

Ingredients:
- 2 tsp. orange zest
- ½ chopped pistachios
- 1 tsp. active yeast
- ½ cup cinnamon sugar mix
- 1 ½ cups lukewarm water
- 1 tsp. salt
- ½ cup dried cranberries
- 3 cups unbleached AP flour

Instructions:
1. First, mix the flour, yeast, salt, water, and sugar together using the bread hook on a stand mixer. For about four minutes, mix on speed 2. Add the orange zest, cranberries, and pistachios, and mix on speed 1 until everything is well mixed.
2. Place in a draft-free area and cover with a clean kitchen towel. Let rise for 10 to 12 hours.
3. Once the proofing period has elapsed, put the dough onto a lightly floured surface and rapidly form a circle. It will be slightly sticky, so flour your hands as well. Do not work the dough too much; just make a rough circle out of it. When the oven and Dutch oven heat up, let the dough rest.
4. To get your Dutch oven ready, put it in an oven with a lid. Warm up to 425° F. Once the Dutch oven has been preheated, remove it from the oven with oven mitts. If you use parchment paper that can handle temperatures up to 425° F, you can pick it up and put it in the Dutch oven. I avoid using parchment paper and instead, place the bread dough directly in the Dutch oven. Do not use silicone or wax paper for baking.
5. Cover and bake for 30-40 minutes. Take the lid off the oven and turn it off. Bake for another 5 to 10 minutes or until golden.
6. Take the bread out of the Dutch oven and let it chill completely on a wire rack for about 10 minutes before serving.
7. After the bread cools, keep it at room temperature for up to three days in a container or sealable bag.
8. I like to eat it with honey and a little ricotta cheese. So tasty!

57. Crusty Apple Cranberry

Prep Time: 15 Minutes / Cook Time: 50 Minutes / Additional Time: 8 Hours / Total Time: 9 Hours 5 Minutes / Yield: 20-24 slices

Ingredients:
- 1/2 cup (60 g) dried cranberries
- 3/4 teaspoon instant yeast
- 1 cup (118 g) diced pink or yellow apples, like gala or fuji
- 1 1/4 teaspoons sea salt
- 2 tablespoons (30 ml) agave nectar
- 1 tablespoon (15 g) cane sugar
- 1 1/2 cups of (355 ml) warm water (under 105 °F)
- 1 teaspoon ground cinnamon
- 2 cups of (273 g) whole wheat flour
- 1/2 cup (55 g) diced pecans
- 2 cups of (277 g) all-purpose flour, plus more for dusting

Instructions:
1. First, mix whole wheat flour, salt, all-purpose flour, and instant yeast together in a large bowl until everything is well mixed. Next, mix warm water and agave nectar with a whisk until the agave melts. Then, add the mixture to the flour.
2. Knead the dough by hand for about 2 minutes, or until there are no dry pockets and the dough is pulling excess flour clean from the sides of the bowl. The mixture may seem a little dry at first, but it will become stickier as you knead it. Cover the bowl with a big plate, a silicone cover, or something else warm, and put it somewhere warm to proof for the first time.
3. To speed up the rise, if my kitchen temperature is below 75F (24C), I turn on my oven light and place the bowl inside (typically 80F or 27C). Depending on the temperature, the loaf will double in size in anywhere from 6 to 10 hours. Take off the cover at that point.
4. Punch out the air in the dough and dust your work surface with flour. First, fold the dough over on itself a few times. Then, make it about 10 inches by 12 inches across. On top, sprinkle with the sugar and cinnamon. Then, evenly spread the apples, cranberries, and pecans out over the top.
5. Starting from a 10-inch (25 cm) side, roll the dough tightly. Then, roll the tube into a spiral, making it into a boule, or use an oval shape. It will depend on the shape of your Dutch oven. For the second proofing, transfer the shaped dough to a very large bowl or deep baking dish lined with parchment paper.
6. Once more, place a cover over the warm area and allow the dough to rise until it doubles in size, which should take about 60 to 90 minutes. While the dough is still rising, heat the oven to 425F (218C) and put the Dutch oven inside.
7. Once the loaf has risen, score a line down the center to allow for expansion, then carefully lift it out of the proofing container by the parchment paper and place it in your Dutch oven. Place the lid on top and bake for 25 minutes. After that, take off the lid and bake for another 25 to 30 minutes, or until the inside is brown and the temperature reaches at least 190F (90C).
8. Once the loaf is done, take it out of the Dutch oven and set it on a rack to cool. Wait to cut into it until it has come to room temperature (this could take several hours). Put it in a bag and keep it at room temperature for up to four days. Then, put it in a refrigerator for up to two weeks. You can also freeze half of it to eat later (in a bag that keeps air out).

58. Lemon Bread with Wild Blueberries

Prep Time: 30 Minutes / Cook Time: 45 Minutes / Additional Time: 1 Hour / Total Time: 2 Hours 10 Minutes / Yield: 20-24 slices

Ingredients:
For the dough:

- 1/2 tsp salt
- 2 tbsp. lemon juice
- 2 cups flour
- 1/4 cup butter, softened
- 1/2 cup warm milk
- 1/4 cup sugar
- 1 packet of active dry yeast
- 2 eggs beaten and divided

For the filling:

- 1/3 cup sugar
- 2 tbsp. lemon zest
- 1 cup dried wild blueberries

Instructions:
1. Mix yeast, milk, two tablespoons of sugar, and lemon juice together. Wait 10 minutes until the yeast blooms or bubbles up.
2. Once the yeast is active, add the remainder of the sugar and salt and mix it in. After that, stir in 1/4 cup beaten eggs and 1/2 cup flour alternately until the mixture is well combined. After that, add the butter and stir. It should be easy to stretch and a little sticky.
3. Next, place the dough in a greased bowl and let it rise for 1 hour.
4. If you're baking at camp, light briquettes and let them burn until they're white hot.

5. Put sugar, blueberries, and lemon zest in a different bowl and mix them together.
6. Press the dough into a big rectangular shape on a flour-filled surface. Cover the dough with the filling mix. Form the dough into a ball and place it in a lightly oiled Dutch oven.
7. Place 7 hot briquettes on the bottom and 15 on top of the Dutch oven. Cook for 45 minutes, turning the lid over two or three times during that time.
8. Take the bread out of the oven. Warm up and serve.

59. No Knead Fig and Walnut Bread

Prep Time: 30 Minutes / Cook Time: 35 Minutes / Additional Time: 1 Day 1 Hour / Total Time: 1 Day 2 Hour 5 Minutes / Yield: 12 slices

Ingredients:
- ½ cup walnuts
- 1 tsp. active dry yeast
- 3½ cups all-purpose flour
- 1½ cups water
- 1 tsp. vanilla extract
- 1 tsp. salt
- 1½ tsp. cinnamon
- ¼ cup honey
- ¾ cup dried figs

Instructions:
1. To make it easier to chop the dried figs, place them in a bowl and cover it with hot water for 10 minutes. Drain, then remove the tough stems and cut them into bite-sized pieces.
2. Warm the oven to 350 degrees F and roast the walnuts for 15 minutes. Cut the walnuts up pretty small.
3. Combine the flour, salt, cinnamon, and yeast in a large glass or ceramic bowl. Add the dried figs and walnuts and mix them in.
4. Heat the water until it is lukewarm, then stir in the vanilla extract and honey until it dissolves.
5. Stir the water mixture into the bowl with a wooden spoon. Mix the flour into the dough until it's all mixed in. It will look like shaggy rugs.
6. Now, tightly wrap it in plastic wrap and place it in a warm area of your kitchen (the oven works well) for at least 6 hours or up to 24 hours. It will double in size and bubble up on top when it's ready.
7. Using the spatula, scrape the dough onto a generously floured surface. Turn the dough over several times with a bench scraper to form it into a ball. Add more flour if you need to at this point.
8. Next, tear a piece of parchment paper big enough to cover your pot's sides and bottom, then carefully lift the dough onto the paper's center. Cover with a tea towel and a little flour. Let it sit for an hour (or even two!).
9. Meanwhile, warm the oven to 450 degrees F. When the oven is heating up, put the Dutch oven in it with the lid on. For 30 minutes, let the oven heat up.
10. Score the bread's top with a sharp knife or bread lame. Cut two to three times as deep as half an inch.
11. Take the Dutch oven out of the oven with great care and remove the lid. It will be very hot! Carefully set the dough in the Dutch oven by lifting it up by the parchment paper's corners. Bake, covered, for 30 minutes.
12. Take off the lid and bake for another 5 to 10 minutes or until the dough reaches 190 to 200 degrees F in the middle.
13. When you remove the lid, if the top of the bread is sufficiently browned, tent it with foil for the remaining baking time.
14. Put it on a wire rack and let it chill completely before cutting.

60. No-Knead Cranberry Bread

Prep Time: 10 Minutes / Cook Time: 45 Minutes / Additional Time: 20 hours / Total Time: 20 Hours 55 Minutes / Yield: 6 slices

Ingredients:
- 3 cups bread flour
- 1 cup dried cranberries
- 1 1/2 cups water
- 1/2 tsp instant yeast
- 1 1/4 tsp salt

Instructions:
1. Put bread flour, salt, and instant yeast in a large bowl. After mixing well, add the water and dried cranberries.
2. Once more, mix it well, and then roll it into a ball. The dough may be lumpy and sticky.
3. Put a cloth over the dough and let it rise for 18 hours.
4. Place the dough in the middle of a big piece of parchment paper. Gently shape the dough into a ball. Place the parchment paper (with the dough on it) in a Dutch oven.
5. Give it two more hours to rise.
6. Let the oven heat up to 450 degrees. For around 30 minutes, bake the bread with the lid on top. After that, take the lid off and bake for another 15 minutes.
7. Allow the bread to chill for around 15 minutes. Serve and enjoy!

61. No-Knead Vegan Cranberry Orange Bread

Prep Time: 35 Minutes / Cook Time: 45 Minutes / Additional Time: 12 hours / Total Time: 13 Hours 20 Minutes / Yield: 10 slices

Ingredients:
- ¼ tsp active dry yeast
- 2 tbsp vital wheat gluten
- ⅓ cup unsalted roasted pumpkin seeds
- 1 cup orange juice
- ½ cup old-fashioned oats
- 2 ½ cups all-purpose flour
- 2 tbsp orange zest
- ½ cup whole wheat flour
- 1 tbsp wheat bran
- ¾ cup lukewarm water
- 1 cup Mariani dried cranberries
- 1 tsp salt

Instructions:
1. First, add whole wheat flour, all-purpose flour, oats, yeast, vital wheat gluten, salt, cranberries, pumpkin seeds, and orange zest in the large mixing bowl. Mix everything together by stirring.
2. Create a well in the center of the mixture and add the ½ cup of lukewarm water and orange juice. Combine until there is no more flour. It should not be dry and crumbly. If it is, add a little more water until all the flour is mixed in and the dough is shaggy and sticky.
3. Place a towel or use plastic wrap over the bowl and allow it for 12 to 18 hours or overnight. Put the bowl in a warm spot to allow the dough to rise.
4. Warm the oven up to 450 degrees.
5. Set the Dutch oven in the oven with the lid on for 30 minutes to heat up. Uncover the dough while the pot heats. When the dough is ready, little air bubbles will cover the top of it. Press down on the dough with your fist and fold it four times over. If it's too sticky, you may need to add a little flour. Let it rise for 30 minutes while the pot heats up. Cover the bowl again.
6. Take out the pot from the oven and remove the lid carefully (wearing two oven mitts). Put a piece of parchment paper inside the pot to make it easier to clean up. Distribute the wheat bran evenly throughout the pot's base.
7. Slide the dough into the pot slowly with a spatula. You'll hear it sizzle right away, so cover it immediately and return the pot to the oven.
8. Cover and bake for 40 minutes. Take the lid off and bake for five more minutes or until the crust is golden brown. Take out the pot from the oven and carefully remove the parchment paper from both sides to remove the bread. Place it on a wire rack and let it cool for an hour before cutting it.

62. Pear, Walnut & Rosemary Bread

Prep Time: 20 Minutes / Cook Time: 45 Minutes / Total Time: 2 Hours 5 Minutes / Yield: 8-10 slices

Ingredients:
- 1 tablespoon nutmeg
- 1 cup of chopped pears
- 1 teaspoon rosemary
- 4 cups of bread flour, plus more for dusting (all-purpose flour)
- 4 ounces unsalted butter, melted
- ¾ teaspoon ground ginger
- ¼ cup chopped walnuts
- 2 tablespoons cinnamon
- 2 teaspoons salt
- 1 cup of warm water (between 110- and 115-degrees F)
- pinch of granulated sugar
- olive oil for topping
- ¼ teaspoon ground cloves
- 2 ¼ teaspoons active dry yeast

Instructions:
1. Heat one cup of water to 110 degrees in a small bowl. Put a pinch of sugar and yeast in the water. Then, give it a quick stir. Set aside for 5 minutes. The mix will start to foam. If it doesn't, start over.
2. Melt the butter in the small pan over medium-low heat. Take it off the heat and add the cloves, cinnamon, nutmeg, rosemary, and ginger. Put away.
3. Using a bread hook attachment, put flour in the bowl of an electric stand mixer. Put salt in. Put in the butter mixture, the activated yeast mixture, the pears, and the walnuts. For 10 minutes, stir slowly. Eventually, the dough will pull almost all the way away from the bottom and clean the sides of the bowl. It's very soft, the dough. Warp the dough in a greased bowl with plastic wrap. Let the dough rise for at least an hour somewhere warm.
4. Warm the oven up to 450 degrees.
5. After that, the dough has doubled in size and is kneaded by hand for two minutes on a floured surface. Grease the bottom of a large Dutch oven with two tablespoons of olive oil. Put the dough in the pot and slice a deep cross into it with a sharp knife. Add three more tablespoons of olive oil on top. Place the lid on top so it fits tightly on top, and bake for 30 minutes. Take the lid off and turn the heat down to 400 degrees. Keep baking for 15 minutes more, until it turns golden brown.

63. Pumpkin Bread

Prep Time: 15 Minutes / Cook Time: 30 Minutes / Additional Time: 12-18 Hours / Total Time: 14-19 Hours / Yield: 20-24 slices

Ingredients:
- 1 cup water
- ¼ cup honey
- ¼ tsp ground cloves
- ½ tsp active dry yeast
- ⅔ cup chopped pecans, toasted
- ¼ tsp ground allspice
- ¾ cup pumpkin purée
- ½ tsp ground cinnamon
- ⅛ tsp nutmeg
- 1 ½ tsp salt
- 3 cups, plus 2 Tbsp bread flour, and more for dusting

Instructions:
1. Add the bread flour, salt, yeast, spices, and toasted pecans to a 2-quart mixing bowl.
2. Put the water, pumpkin purée, and honey in a small bowl. Make sure to stir the mix until it's smooth.
3. Bring the pumpkin mixture into the flour mixture and mix it in until it is fully absorbed. Put plastic wrap over the bowl and let the dough rise for 12-18 hours.
4. Place the dough on a surface dusted with a lot of flour and roll it into a ball. Transfer the dough onto a parchment paper sheet. Warp the dough with plastic wrap and put it back in the bowl. Let it rise for an hour.
5. Set oven temperature to 450°. After the oven reaches temperature, put a covered Dutch oven in the oven for around 30 minutes.
6. After taking the hot pot out of the oven, carefully lift the dough into the pot using the parchment paper and place it there.
7. After covering the pot, put it back in the oven for thirty minutes.
8. After taking the bread out of the oven, let it cool on a rack for 10-15 minutes or until you can't wait another minute.

VEGETABLE BREADS

64. Cheddar Potato Bread

Prep Time: 10 Minutes / Cook Time: 35 Minutes / Resting Time: 12 Hours / Total Time: 12 Hours 45 Minutes / Yield: 12-16 slices

Ingredients:
- 3/4 cup (50g) dried potato flakes
- 1/2 tsp. (1.5g) active yeast
- 3 cups (about 1 lb.) flour
- 2 cups (8 oz) shredded sharp cheddar cheese
- 2 tsp. (18 g) salt
- 1 3/4 cups (14oz) warm water

Instructions:
1. Pour water into a large bowl and stir in the flour, salt, yeast, and potato flakes. Do this for about 20 seconds.
2. Add the shredded cheese.
3. Mix the dry ingredients in until they are all mixed in. It will be pretty thick. Keep mixing. Don't add water because it will thin the dough and make it hard to shape into a ball after it has risen.
4. Take the bowl out of the fridge and cover it with plastic wrap.
5. Up to eight to twelve hours later, the dough will have doubled in size and a lot of tiny bubbles on top.
6. Spread the dough out on a floured surface. To make a ball, fold the ends together. Flip the dough over so that the folded side is facing down. Put on a piece of parchment paper to make it easy to lift. Rest for 20 to 30 minutes.
7. Warm up the Dutch oven in an oven set to 450°F for 20 to 30 minutes.
8. After letting the bread rest, make a cut in the top with a "x" or any other design you like to let steam out.
9. Once the Dutch oven is hot, carefully take it out of the oven. Place the bread dough ball on parchment paper in the Dutch oven. COVER with a lid.
10. Cover and bake at 450°F for 25 minutes. Then lower heat to 425°F and bake without the lid for another 10 to 15 minutes, or until the crust is golden brown and the center temperature reaches 195°F or higher.
11. Take the bread out of the Dutch oven when it's done and let it cool for at least an hour before cutting it.

65. No Knead Potato Bread

Prep Time: 10 Minutes / Cook Time: 50 Minutes / Resting Time: 1 Hour / Total Time: 2 Hours / Yield: 16 slices

Ingredients:
- 4½ cups all-purpose flour
- 2 cups warm water
- 12 ounces potatoes
- 1 teaspoon salt
- 1 tablespoon active dry yeast

Instructions:
1. Make sure all of the potatoes are cut into equal-sized pieces so that they all cook at the same time. Toss the potatoes in a big pot with cold water until they are completely covered. Add a teaspoon of salt to the water and stir it around.
2. Over high heat, bring potatoes to boil. Then, lower the heat to medium and cook for about 15 minutes, or until the potatoes are soft enough to pierce with a fork.
3. After draining the potatoes, you can use a potato masher or a ricer to mash them.
4. Combine the flour, mashed potatoes, salt, and yeast in a large bowl. Use spatula or wooden spoon, mix the water into the bowl until it's well mixed in.
5. Put plastic wrap over the bowl and leave it on the counter or in an oven that isn't hot for an hour, until it has doubled in size.
6. Heat the oven up to 450°F. Warm up your 6-quart Dutch oven in the oven while it's heating up, too, until it reaches 450°F. When the oven is ready, the pot should usually be hot enough too. Carefully take the pot out of the oven and remove the lid. Protect yourself from getting burned by using oven mitts.
7. Lightly dust your hands with flour and place some on top of the dough. With floured hands, take the dough out of the bowl slowly and shape it into a rough ball on a surface that has been dusted with flour. On a piece of parchment paper, put your dough ball. Put some pepitas or sunflower seeds on top of the bread if you want to.
8. Place the whole piece of parchment paper, including the paper, in the pot.
9. Place in the oven with the lid on for 30 minutes. Take it off and bake for another 15 to 20 minutes, or until top is golden brown. The bread should just fall out of the pot when you take it out. Let it cool down all the way before cutting it up and serving.

66. Onion Yeast Bread

Prep Time: 15 Minutes / Cook Time: 40 Minutes / Resting Time: 1 Hour 15 Minutes / Total Time: 2 Hours 10 Minutes / Yield: 12 slices

Ingredients:
- 1 egg
- 1 ½ teaspoons dried minced onion
- 3 teaspoons olive oil
- 2 tablespoons sugar
- 1 package rapid rise yeast
- 1 ½ teaspoons poppy seed
- 1 ½ teaspoons dried minced garlic
- 1 tablespoon butter
- 3 1/2 cups all-purpose flour plus additional for kneading
- 1 tablespoon water
- 2 cups warm water
- ¼ cup fresh minced yellow onion
- 2 teaspoons salt

Instructions:
1. Put the poppy seeds, garlic, and onion in a small bowl and mix them together. Set aside.
2. Put the onion and butter in a pan. Cook over medium heat until the onions get tender. Set aside.
3. Now, combine the yeast, sugar, and water in a large bowl, then mix them together using a whisk. Wait a few minutes until it starts to foam up.
4. Add the onion, salt, and olive oil, and mix them together. Stir the flour in slowly until it's all mixed in. If you need to, add more flour to make soft dough that isn't too sticky. Leave it in a warm place with the lid on for about 45 minutes to an hour, or until it has almost doubled in size.
5. Place the dough on a floured surface and knead it a few times to make the outside less sticky and lightly coat it with flour. To make a loaf, roll out the dough and cut it into three equal pieces.
6. Make a long strand out of each piece and then braid them together. Put on a baking sheet that has been greased or in a Dutch oven that is 10 to 12 inches wide (circle the dough around the oven).
7. Put a towel over it and let it rise again for 30 to 45 minutes.
8. In a small cup, mix the egg and water together with a whisk. Use a little of the egg mixture to brush the top of the loaf. Add the poppy seed mix on top.
9. Heat the oven up to 375 degrees F and bake the bread for about 40 minutes, or until the top is light golden brown and the bread sounds hollow when tapped. You can serve it hot or cold.

67. Sweet Potato Bread

Prep Time: 20 Minutes / Cook Time: 40 Minutes / Resting Time: 5 Hours / Total Time: 6 Hours / Yield: 12-16 slices

Ingredients:
- 1¼ cups (284 grams) warm water (105°F/41°C to 110°F/43°C)
- 1½ cups (380 grams) lightly mashed baked sweet potato (see Note)
- 4 cups (508 grams) bread flour
- 1 tablespoon (9 grams) kosher salt
- 2¼ teaspoons (7 grams) instant yeast
- Corn flour, for dusting

Instructions:
1. Put yeast, salt, sweet potato, and bread flour in a large bowl. Add ¼ cup (284 grams) of warm water and mix it in by hand until it's all mixed in and a sticky dough form. You could also put the yeast, salt, sweet potato, bread flour, and stand mixer bowl with the paddle attachment in it. Add ½ cup (284 grams) of warm water and beat on them medium speed for at least 30 seconds, or wait until a sticky dough forms.
2. Cover and let rise for two hours at 75°F/24°C in a warm, draft-free area. Then, put it in the fridge for at least two hours, preferably overnight.
3. Place the dough on a lightly floured surface and press it down just enough to make it level. Fold the dough edges toward the center, pressing lightly, beginning on the left side and working clockwise. To make dough, flip the ball over and cup and pull the dough toward you with both hands. Repeat until you have a round of dough that is smooth, tight, and sealed.
4. Sprinkle a lot of corn flour on a piece of parchment paper. Place the dough on the paper, seam side up. Cover and set aside in a warm, draft-free place (75°F/24°C) for 1 hour.
5. It's time for the dough to rise. Put the 6- to 7-quart Dutch oven and lid in a cold oven. Warm the oven up to 260°F (500°C).
6. Carefully take the hot Dutch oven out of the oven, take off the lid, and quickly place the bread inside the Dutch oven so that the seam is on the bottom. Score the top of the bread. Put the dish back in the oven and cover it with the lid.
7. Lower the oven's temperature right away to 450°F (230°C). Bake for twenty-five minutes. Take off the lid and then you need to bake for another 10 to 15 minutes, or wait until an instant-read thermometer reads 190°F (88°C) is inserted in the middle. Take the loaf out of the Dutch oven right away and place it on a wire rack to cool completely.

68. Tomato Basil Bread

Prep Time: 15 Minutes / Cook Time: 45 Minutes / Resting Time: 12 Hours / Total Time: 13 Hours / Yield: 12 slices

Ingredients:
- 1/2 teaspoon active dry yeast
- 1/2 cup chopped sun-dried tomatoes (not in oil)
- 1 tablespoon dried basil
- 1 teaspoon salt
- 1-3/4 cups lukewarm water
- 3 cups unbleached all-purpose flour

Instructions:
1. Put everything in a big bowl and stir it around until everything is well mixed. It's going to be very wet. Take the bowl and wrap it in plastic wrap. Leave it at room temperature for at least 12 hours or overnight.
2. Place your dough on a surface that has been lightly floured. Add some flour to the dough then fold it over on itself a few times. Put a light dish towel over the top and let it rise for two hours.
3. Warm the oven up to 450 F, then put a 3- to 5-quart Dutch oven in it to heat up. How thick your bread is in the middle will depend on size of the Dutch oven you use. For thicker loaves, use a smaller Dutch oven, and for thinner loaves, use a larger Dutch oven. Change the baking time as needed.
4. Take Dutch oven off the heat carefully and coat the inside with some olive oil. Put the dough in the Dutch oven, cover it, and bake it for 30 minutes. Take off the lid after 30 minutes and bake for another 10 to 15 minutes. Allow to cool and then cut.

69. Zucchini Bread

Prep Time: 20 Minutes / Cook Time: 60 Minutes / Total Time: 1 Hour 20 Minutes / Yield: 12 slices

Ingredients:
- 1 teaspoon ground cinnamon
- 2 teaspoons baking soda
- 2/3 cup melted butter plus butter to grease pan
- 1 teaspoon sea salt
- 3 cups zucchini shredded
- 4 eggs
- 1 1/2 cup coconut sugar
- 2 teaspoons pure vanilla extract
- 3 cups whole wheat pastry flour
- 1/2 cup coarsely chopped nuts
- 1/2 teaspoon baking powder
- 1/2 teaspoon ground cloves

Instructions:
1. Preheat a Dutch oven with legs by placing 15 hot coals on top of lid and 7 hot coals evenly spaced under the pot to bring a Dutch oven to 350°F. If it gets cold, add a few more briquettes.
2. Using softened butter, grease the bottom of the Dutch oven.
3. In a large bowl, mix together the eggs, vanilla, coconut sugar, melted butter, and zucchini.
4. Now, combine rest of the ingredients, mix them in, and then pour the mixture into a Dutch oven that has already been heated.
5. Place in the oven and bake for about 50 to 60 minutes, or wait until a wooden pick stuck in the middle comes out clean.
6. Now, let it cool for at least 10 minutes. To make the bread easier to handle, run a knife along the sides. Flip the Dutch oven over by putting a dish on top of it. We can now put the cake on the plate.
7. Let it cool down before cutting.

SWEET BREADS

70. Cinnamon Monkey Bread

Prep Time: 15 Minutes / Cook Time: 30 Minutes / Total Time: 45 Minutes / Yield: 8 slices

Ingredients:
- 2 rolls of Pillsbury biscuits
- ½ cup brown sugar
- ½ cup sugar
- 1 stick butter, melted
- 3 Tbsp cinnamon

Instructions:
1. Apply cooking spray to the Dutch oven. Put foil inside the oven and spray it with cooking spray.
2. Chop the biscuits into quarters. Use a plastic bag to mix the sugar and cinnamon. Place each quarter in the bag and shake to coat well.
3. Then put the mix in the Dutch oven.
4. Melt the butter in a different pan, then pour it over the biscuits.
5. Bake at 350°F for 35 minutes. After about 30 minutes, check to see if the dough is done.

71. Double Chocolate No-Knead Bread

Prep Time: 15 Minutes / Cook Time: 50 Minutes / Total Time: 1 Hour 5 Minutes / Yield: 8 slices

Ingredients:
- 3/4 cup (134 g) dairy-free chocolate chips or chocolate chunks
- 3 cups (405 g) all-purpose flour
- 1/4 cup (18 g) cocoa or cacao powder
- 1 1/2 cups (355 ml) + 2 tablespoons room temperature water, divided
- 1 teaspoon kosher salt
- 1/2 teaspoon active dry yeast or instant yeast (I used reg)
- 2 tablespoons cane sugar

Instructions:
1. First, sift the cocoa powder into the flour in a large bowl. Add the yeast, sugar, and salt, and then mix them well with a whisk. Cut a hole in the middle of the dough, then add the water and mix it with a wooden spoon. If there is any flour left in the dough after it starts to get thicker, add chocolate chips and mix well until all the flour is gone. If the dough is too dry, add the extra 2 tablespoons of water. The dough will be thick and lumpy. Place the bowl aside and allow it to rest for 12 to 18 hours after covering it with plastic wrap.

2. Set oven's temperature to 450 degrees Fahrenheit. After that, place a coated 6-quart (or comparable-sized) Dutch oven inside the oven and let it heat for half an hour. Set aside a sheet of parchment paper.
3. After resting for a full night, the dough ought to look extremely loose and bubbly and have at least doubled in size. Transfer the dough to a well-floured surface with a spatula right before baking. Also, dust your hands with flour. Pull bottom edges of the dough ball towards the middle of the top, pinching the dough together firmly to "shape" it. Remember not to knead it! Repeat several times until you have a tight ball, then flip the ball onto the parchment paper sheet. Usually, I do this right before I take it out of the oven.
4. Carefully take the hot Dutch oven out of the oven and put the dough and parchment paper inside. Cover the oven and put it back in. After baking for 30 minutes with the lid on, take off the lid and bake for another 18 to 20 minutes to get a nice, crispy crust.
5. Remove it from the oven and put it on a rack to cool. Wait until it's cool to cut or cut it up while it's still warm and the chocolate chips are still soft.

72. Honey Oat Artisan Bread

Prep Time: 20 Minutes / Cook Time: 40 Minutes / Raising Time: 2 Hours / Total Time: 3 Hours / Yield: 12-16 slices

Ingredients:
- ✓ 3 ½ cups bread flour
- ✓ 1 packet of active dry yeast
- ✓ 1 cup old fashioned oats + more for topping
- ✓ 3 tablespoon honey
- ✓ 2 cups water - warm
- ✓ 1 ½ teaspoon salt

Instructions:
1. First, combine warm water and honey in a small bowl. Set aside.
2. Combine the flour, oats, yeast, and salt in a large bowl, then mix them together using a whisk.
3. Incorporate the honey water into the dry ingredients. Give it a good stir, cover with a towel or plastic wrap, then allow it to rise for two hours.
4. Place bread dough on floured parchment. Form the dough into a circular loaf. Put more oats on top, and then cover again for 30 minutes.
5. Set the Dutch oven inside the oven and heat it up to 420 degrees F.
6. When the oven reaches the temperature, carefully remove Dutch oven and place bread dough inside (wrapped in parchment paper). Put the lid on and bake for 30 minutes.
7. Take the lid off after 30 minutes and bake for another 5 to 10 minutes or until the crust is golden.
8. Remove the Dutch oven with care, then you need to set the bread on a wire rack to cool completely.

73. No-Knead Chocolate Chip Bread

Prep Time: 15 Minutes / Cook Time: 1 Hour / Total Time: 1 Hour 15 Minutes / Yield: 12 slices

Ingredients:
- ✓ 1 cup semi-sweet chocolate chips
- ✓ 4 1/2 cups bread flour + 1/2 cup for dusting
- ✓ 2 tsp cinnamon
- ✓ 2 1/4 cups warm water (105-115 degrees F)
- ✓ 1 1/2 tsp salt
- ✓ 1 1/2 tsp active dry yeast

Instructions:
1. Add the yeast, salt, and flour to a large bowl and stir to mix. Put the water on top of the mixture and stir it with a wooden spoon until dough starts to form. The dough will be very sticky.
2. Place the bowl on the counter (do not put it in the fridge) and cover it tightly with plastic wrap. Leave it there for 8 to 18 hours. During that time, the dough will rise and slowly flatten out, making bubbles on top. Please keep in mind that the dough will at least double in size before you pick it up.
3. Now, heat the oven to 450 degrees and put a 6-quart Dutch oven in it. At the same time, add the cinnamon and chocolate chips to the dough and quickly knead or stir the dough to spread the chocolate chips and cinnamon out. Put the last 1/2 cup of flour on top of the dough and roll it into a ball. There will be stickiness! Then, put the ball on a piece of parchment paper and set it aside for at least 15 minutes while the oven heats up.
4. Put the bread in the Dutch oven with the parchment paper still on it, cover it, and bake for forty-five minutes. Take the cover off the bread and bake it for another 15 minutes or until the dough is baked through.
5. Wait 20 minutes (if you can!) before cutting the bread.

74. No-Knead Cranberry Pecan Bread

Prep Time: 5 Minutes / Cook Time: 35 Minutes / Rise Time: 18 Hours / Total Time: 18 Hours 40 Minutes / Yield: 12 slices

Ingredients:
- 3 1/4 cups (400g) Bread Flour
- 1 1/2 cups Warm Water 110 degrees or cooler
- 3/4 cup (105g) Dried Cranberries or Dried Cherries
- 1/4 tsp (1g) Instant Yeast
- 3 tsp (20g) Sea Salt
- 3/4 cup (95g) Chopped Pecans or Chopped Walnuts
- 1 tbsp (10g) Maple Syrup

Instructions:
1. In a large bowl or dough bucket, mix the flour, salt, yeast, pecans, cranberries, and maple syrup. Mix in the warm water until everything is well mixed. It will be very sticky and wet. Make a ball out of the dough, or at least something that looks like a round shape, and cover the bowl tightly with plastic wrap. If you're using a bucket, you can secure the lid. Let it rise for 12 to 18 hours at room temperature. Also, the dough will get very wet and start to bubble up during that time.
2. Spread some flour on a lightly floured surface and roll the dough into a ball. Place the dough on a large piece of parchment paper that can handle high temperatures. Use a sharp knife to make an X in the top of the dough. Making cuts in the dough helps the bread rise evenly while it's baking.
3. Put some plastic wrap around the dough and let it rest for 30 minutes. Set the oven to 475°F and put your Dutch oven with the lid in it to heat up while the dough rests. After 30 minutes, carefully take the pot out of the oven, add the dough with the parchment paper, and put the lid on top. Bake for twenty-five minutes. Take the lid off and bake the bread for another 8 to 10 minutes, until it's a nice golden-brown color. After taking the pot out of the oven, carefully take the bread out of the pot by lifting the parchment paper. Let the loaf cool for 30 minutes on the counter or a rack before cutting it.

75. No-Knead Sweet Cinnamon Bread

Prep Time: 5 Minutes / Cook Time: 30 Minutes / Resting Time: 3 Hours / Total Time: 3 Hours 35 Minutes / Yield: 12-16 slices

Ingredients:
- 50g butter
- 1/2 cup brown sugar
- 1 egg
- 1 teaspoon cinnamon
- 1 and 1/2 cups hot water
- 1/4 teaspoon salt
- 1/2 teaspoon dried yeast
- 3 cups all-purpose flour

Instructions:
1. Shortly heat up 50g of butter in the microwave.
2. Mix all-purpose flour, brown sugar, salt, and dried yeast in a large bowl. Mix the hot water in until it's all mixed in. Add one egg, lightly beaten, to the dough.
3. Put cling film over it and let it sit for at least three hours.
4. Before you start, prepare your Dutch oven by lining a bowl with parchment paper. Now, turn dough out onto a lightly dusted surface and you need to roll it into a ball. Place it in the prepared bowl, then cover it with cling film, and set aside to rest. Simply put the Dutch oven in the cold oven and set the temperature to 220°.
5. Now, after 30 minutes, take the Dutch oven out of the oven carefully, put the dough inside, and cover it. Let it bake for 30 minutes. If you think it needs more color, take the lid off and bake it for 5 more minutes.
6. Give it some time to cool down before you cut it!

76. Sweet Honey Cornbread

Prep Time: 5 Minutes / Cook Time: 45 Minutes / Total Time: 50 Minutes / Yield: 12 slices

Ingredients:
- 2 cups flour
- ¾ tsp salt
- 1 ¾ cups milk
- ¼ cup cooking oil like avocado oil, vegetable oil, or canola oil
- 3 eggs beaten
- 2 TBS honey
- ½ cup melted butter
- 1 cup cornmeal
- 1 ½ TBS baking powder
- 1 cup sugar

Instructions:
1. In a big bowl, mix cornmeal, flour, sugar, baking powder, and salt.
2. Mix in the milk, eggs, honey, butter, oil, and butter. Add water and stir until just combined. The mixture may still have some lumps.
3. Heat the oven to 375 to 425 degrees.
4. Place Dutch oven in the oven to heat it up. Spread some oil around the inside.
5. Cover the dish after pouring the batter into it.
6. Now, cover and bake in the oven for 20 to 30 minutes. Check every 5 to 10 minutes to make sure the middle is done. Take off the cover for the last few minutes if you want more of the golden-brown top.
7. Serve with honey and butter after cutting into wedges or squares.

SOURDOUGH BREADS

77. Beetroot Sourdough Bread

Prep Time: 30 Minutes / Cook Time: 45 Minutes / Resting Time: 4 Hours 20 Minutes / Total Time: 5 Hours 35 Minutes / Yield: 18 slices

Ingredients:
- 400g rye flour
- 430g raw beetroot, coarsely grated
- 670g water
- 1kg all-purpose (plain) flour
- 18g salt

Instructions:
1. Mix flour, water, and rye flour in a large bowl. For 20 to 30 minutes, let it autolyze.
2. Add the salt and beetroot. Incorporate by kneading. You can leave the bowl on the counter for 4 hours with a damp tea towel or cling film over it. Stretch and fold the dough several times during this time. Grab a piece of dough, lift it, and fold it back on itself while it is still in the bowl. Turn the bowl a little and repeat the stretch, and fold again. Do it several times.
3. When the dough has risen about a third of the way, turn it out onto a lightly floured surface, split it in half, and roll each half into a ball. Take a 20-minute break.
4. Once they have rested, shape them again into "boules." Transfer to well-floured bowls or bannetons. Proof for two hours.
5. Set your Dutch oven on the middle shelf of the oven and heat it to its highest setting.
6. After scoring the first loaf, cover the Dutch oven and bake for 30 minutes. Take the lid off, lower the heat to 230°C, and bake for another 15 minutes.
7. Moving carefully to a wire rack, let it rest for at least an hour. Do the same thing with the other loaf.

78. Carrot Raisin Sourdough Bread

Prep Time: 15 Minutes / Cook Time: 35 Minutes / Resting Time: 4 Hours / Total Time: 4 Hours 50 Minutes / Yield: 18-20 slices

Ingredients:
- 770 Grams Water Room temperature
- 1000 Grams Bread Flour
- 20 Grams Salt Fine
- 200 Grams Levain (Ripe sourdough starter)
- 170 Grams Grated Carrots
- 200 Grams Raisins Weighed before soaked
- Rice Flour Just enough to sprinkle inside the bannetons to prevent the dough from sticking.

Instructions:
1. Let the raising soak overnight.
2. Measure out all of the ingredients before you start mixing the dough.
3. In a bowl, mix the sourdough starter, water, and flour. Mix it well with your hands, making sure there are no dry spots. Then, set it aside for 30 minutes.
4. After the 30 minutes are up, add the salt.
5. After you've mixed in the salt, add the raisins and carrots. Mix everything together until it's all mixed in. Leave the dough at room temperature for 30 minutes with plastic wrap over it.
6. For the next three hours, perform folds every thirty minutes.
7. Divide your loaf in half, shape it, and place it in your bannetons. I like to put rice flour in my bannetons so the dough doesn't stick.
8. After deflating the loaf, if it's still not filling up the banneton, leave it at room temperature until it rises to the right level.
9. After that, put your loaves in the fridge for at least 12 hours and no more than 48 hours to let the magic happen!
10. In your Dutch Oven, bake at 475°F for 20 minutes. Make sure the lid stays on for 20 minutes. Then take it off and bake for another 10 minutes, or until you like the color of the crust.

79. Cocoa Chocolate Cherry Sourdough Bread

Prep Time: 20 Minutes / Cook Time: 40 Minutes / Total Time: 60 Minutes / Yield: 8 slices

Ingredients:
- 225 grams (1 2/3 cup) bread flour
- 230 grams (1 cup + 1 Tbsp) sourdough starter, ripe or discard
- 30 grams cocoa powder 1/4 cup
- 7 grams salt
- 100 grams dried cherries, sweetened or unsweetened 1 cup
- 150 grams dark chocolate chips or small chunks 1 cup
- 1 tsp espresso powder
- 4 grams (1 tsp.) instant yeast
- 185 grams (3/4 cup) warm water

Instructions:
1. Stir the sourdough starter, warm water, and yeast together in a large bowl by your hand or with a stand mixer fitted with a dough hook. Combine the cocoa powder, espresso powder, and bread flour. Mix until you have a big, shaggy ball. Leave it alone for 30 minutes with the cover on.
2. Pour in the salt. Once thoroughly combined, transfer the dough to an oiled, coverable bowl. Cover and take 30 minutes to rest.
3. Before you bake it, fold it four times. Rest for 30 minutes. Combine the dried cherries and chocolate chips. Dried cherries tend to stick together, so make sure you break them up first. Rest for 30 minutes and fold.
4. Again, fold and rest for 30 minutes FOUR times. Which means this is SIX folds. After the last fold, rest for another 30 minutes. This is done to make gluten.
5. At this point, you can either leave it as one loaf or cut it in half. Cover the dough well (so that the seam side is still facing up) and put it in the fridge for 14 hours.
6. Insert a piece of parchment paper into your Dutch oven now. Place the dough in the Dutch oven so that the rounded side is facing up. Cover and let it sit at room temperature for one to two hours.
7. As the time runs out, heat the oven to 500 degrees. Indent the sourdough's top with a knife. Like a cross or hashtag, this should be 1/4" to 1/2" high on top.
8. Lower the heat to 450 degrees and place the Dutch oven FACE UP in the middle of the oven or on the upper rack, as high as it can go.
9. It needs 33 minutes at 450°F.
10. Pull the lid off and bake for 5 minutes.
11. Unlock the oven door and bake for five more minutes.
12. Take the Dutch oven out of the oven. Carefully move the bread and parchment paper to a wire rack.
13. It tastes great on its own or with butter. Once it's completely cool, put it in a sealed plastic bag and keep it at room temperature.

80. Cherry Seeded Sourdough Bread

Prep Time: 10 Minutes / Cook Time: 45 Minutes / Rest Time: 10 Hours / Total Time: 10 Hours 55 Minutes / Yield: 12 slices

Ingredients:
- 3 tablespoons poppy seeds
- 55 grams active sourdough starter at its peak
- 370 grams slightly warmer than room temperature water
- 50 grams whole-wheat flour
- 1/2 cup raw sunflower seeds
- 15 grams honey
- 360 grams bread flour
- 9 grams fine sea salt
- 90 grams dried Montmorency tart cherries
- 90 grams unbleached all-purpose flour

Instructions:
1. With a fork, mix the starter, water, and honey in a large bowl until the starter is dispersed. Mix in the flour with a spatula first. Then, use your hands to mix it until you get a shaggy dough that doesn't show any flour. Add salt to the top.
2. Use the autolyse method: put a damp cloth over it and let it sit for 45 minutes.
3. Do your first set of stretch and folds while working with salt. Now wait 30 minutes and do another set. You should wait 30 minutes before adding the Montmorency tart cherries. After 30 minutes, do your last set of stretch and folds, which is your 4th set.
4. After doing the stretching and folding for two hours, you will let the dough finish fermenting in its bulk. For example, if your house is 72 degrees, leave the dough to rise on the counter for four to five hours. It could take longer or shorter depending on the temperature.
5. After bulk fermentation, the dough should be doubled in size and look puffy and jiggly. The presence of small bubbles on the sides and on top is proof that the fermentation process is going well.
6. Place the dough on a surface that has been lightly floured. Keep the dough there for 10 to 15 minutes.
7. Then, flatten the dough.
8. On a flat plate, get your seeds ready. Brush the top and sides of your dough with water. Put the dough's top side gently on top of the seeds, and then roll the dough back and forth to stick the seeds together.
9. Once the dough is shaped, use a bench scraper to place it seam-side up on a floured banneton. So, the top with the seeds will be at the bottom of the banneton.
10. Place a damp cloth over it and let it rise one last time on the counter. If your house is about 70 degrees, this will take at least 1 1/2 to 2 hours. OR, you can put the banneton in a plastic bag and leave it there overnight to rise. Now, the dough can stay in the fridge for about 10 hours.
11. Now, preheat your oven and Dutch oven to 500 degrees F once your dough has completed its final rise, risen slightly, and become puffy on top. If you want to know if your dough is ready, press your floured thumb gently into it.
12. When the oven is ready, put parchment paper on top of the dough and flip it over so that the seam side is on the paper. This will let you score the top of the dough.
13. Using a bread lame, score the dough in a few spots that are at least 1/2 inch deep to allow dough to release its gases. You won't get any rise from your bread after that.
14. Putting the dough on the parchment paper and covering it with a Dutch oven lid. Lower the oven's temperature to 450 degrees F. then, cover and bake at 450 degrees F for 20 minutes.
15. After 25 more minutes, take off the lid, lower the heat to 430 degrees F, and bake the bread until it is golden brown and crackly.
16. Take it out of the oven and put it on a rack to cool. Wait at least 1 hour before cutting. It will be squished and sticky if you don't.

81. Chocolate-Cherry Sourdough Bread

Prep Time: 12 Minutes / Cook Time: 48 Minutes / Rest Time: 15 Hours / Total Time: 16 Hours / Yield: 10 slices

Ingredients:
- 1 cup chocolate, roughly chopped
- 2 1/4 cups bread flour
- 1/2 cup active sourdough starter (100% hydration)
- 3/4 cup water
- 1 1/8 teaspoons salt
- 1 cup dried tart cherry
- 3 tablespoons water

Instructions:
1. The night before, try to dissolve the starter in water. Combine the flour and salt.
2. Combine the flour with the starter slurry and mix it all together until it's all hydrated. The dough should be very tacky and slightly sticky but not overly so.
3. Cover bowl with plastic or a plate, and leave it at room temperature (roughly 70°F) for 12 hours (anywhere from 10 to 14 hours is fine).
4. Add some hot water to the cherries. While tart cherries aren't always available, dried cranberries will usually work just as well. After soaking the fruit for about 15 minutes, drain it and lay it out on paper towels or towels to dry.
5. Add the chocolate and cherries to a bowl and mix it all together.
6. Lightly flour a work surface, and then carefully move the dough out onto it. Form the dough into a rectangle by pressing it down lightly with wet hands. Twice as long as it started, spread out 1/4 of the chocolate cherry mixture in the middle of the dough. Spread another quarter of the mixture on top and then fold one-third of the dough on top of that. After turning the dough over one quarter, fold the last third of it in half like a letter. After doing the same thing, cover the dough. Take a rest for about 15 minutes.
7. After letting the dough rest for around 15 minutes, gently roll it into a boule shape and put it in a banneton that has been lightly floured.
8. Let it rise for three hours.
9. Set oven to 500°F and put in my cloche, a Dutch oven, a casserole that can go in the oven, a baking stone, or a baking sheet.
10. Score the bread and bake it for 30 minutes (covered if possible) and then for 17 to 18 minutes (uncovered) for a total of 48 minutes. Wait for it to cool.

82. Honey, Blue Cheese and Walnut Sourdough

Prep Time: 18 Minutes / Cook Time: 42 Minutes / Total Time: 60 Minutes / Yield: 12-16 slices

Ingredients:
- 260g water
- 120g walnuts
- 60g honey
- 10g sea salt
- 135g blue cheese
- 400g strong flour
- 180g levain

Instructions:
1. To make the levain, this needs to be done eight to ten hours before you make the dough. Mix together 60g of sourdough starter, 60g of strong white flour (or rye flour if you're using a rye starter), and 60g of water. Cover and let it sit at room temperature until you're ready to start making the dough.
2. To make a rough dough, mix the flour and water together in a clean bowl. Add the loose flour and mix it all in until it's all mixed in. Don't do anything with the dough for 30 minutes; just let it sit at room temperature.
3. Add the salt, honey, and levain to the dough after 30 minutes of autolyse. Knead the dough for about two to three minutes. It's okay that the dough is wet and sticky; don't add any more flour. The kneading can be done in the bowl, so there's no need to move the dough to the counter. Let the dough rest for 10 minutes after 2 to 3 minutes.
4. Knead the dough again for one minute after taking a ten-minute break. You can see that the dough has already started to rise just by giving it a break. Move the dough to a clean bowl that has been greased. Let the dough rest for 30 minutes.
5. Fold and stretch. Every 30 minutes, we want to stretch and fold our dough to make it stronger. We'll do this twice, with a 30-minute break in between each fold. Now is the best time to add the walnuts and blue cheese. After the second stretch and fold, just let the dough rise for another four hours before you shape it. While the dough is being stretched out, sprinkle some blue cheese and walnuts on top of it. Turn the dough over. After going back to the bowl, rest for 30 minutes and then do it again.
6. Allow the dough to rise for four hours, then turn it out onto a floured surface. Shape the dough ahead of time without knocking out too much air. Now, allow the dough to rest on the counter for about ten minutes.
7. You should dust it with flour before proving it, whether you use a proving basket, a Pyrex dish, or

just a bowl lined with a tea towel. You can use rice flour or rye flour.

8. Spread flour over the dough's surface and shape it into a round shape. Place the round shape into your proving basket with the seam side up. Place shaped dough in a warm place to rise for 30 minutes. Then, put it in the fridge to rise overnight.
9. Take the dough out of the fridge the next day. Preheat the oven to 240c and put an empty baking sheet in the bottom of it.
10. Take the dough out of the proving basket, sprinkle it with flour, and then make cuts in it. Put the dome on top of the dough and bake it in a Dutch oven.
11. Put it in the oven for 35 minutes with the lid on and 8 more minutes without it. In a Dutch oven, you don't need to steam the bread. If you're just baking on a baking tray, you do need to add steam to the oven. Putting boiling water on the tray that is already hot in the base of your oven is one way to do this.

83. Lemon Blueberry Sourdough Bread

Prep Time: 30 Minutes / Cook Time: 35 Minutes / Resting Time: 18 Hours / Total Time: 19 Hours 5 Minutes / Yield: 24 slices

Ingredients:
- 230 grams all-purpose flour
- 70 grams whole wheat flour
- 320 grams water (divided)
- 80 grams ripe starter
- 10 grams fine sea salt
- 100 grams bread flour
- Zest of 2 large lemons
- 1 cup fresh blueberries (rinsed, drained well, and patted dry with paper towels)

Instructions:
1. Mix the flour and 310 grams of water together in a large bowl (Make sure the water is at room temperature.) Just mix until the flour soaks up all the water. Put plastic wrap over it and let it rest for 20 minutes to 6 hours. (90 minutes is a good time.)
2. You can use a Danish dough whisk or your wet hands to mix in the starter. Pour the last 10 grams of water over the top and sprinkle the salt on top. Use a clawing motion with your hands to mix the salt and water together completely. Knead dough in the bowl by folding it over and punching it into the other dough with your fist while turning the bowl all the time. Do this until the dough is not sticky and is all the same size. Keep your hands slightly wet while you knead it because it will be sticky.
3. You should let the bulk ferment for three to three and a half hours and do three sets of four folds at 60, 90, and 120 minutes. For the first fold, add ¼ of the blueberries and lemon zest right before each fold. (Wait 30 minutes more and do another set of folds if the dough feels dry.)
4. Shape the dough ahead of time on a lightly floured surface, then leave it alone for 30 minutes to rest.
5. Shape the dough into the shape you want, then put it into a banneton that has been lightly dusted with rice flour. Before you put the dough into the banneton, make sure to stretch the outside of it. Wait 20 minutes without covering the dough.
6. Cover banneton with plastic wrap and put it in the fridge for 12 to 18 hours.
7. Preheat oven to 500° F and put in the Dutch oven.
8. Before you bake the bread, take the banneton out of the fridge then, remove plastic wrap. Cover the banneton with parchment paper. Then, put a cutting board on top of the paper. Turn it over and lift the banneton off of it. (If the bread is stuck to the banneton, try to loosen it up slowly.)
9. Score the bread as desired. Take the Dutch oven out of the oven, open it up, and carefully place the parchment paper inside the hot Dutch oven. Spray the bread with water or add three ice cubes and cover the Dutch oven immediately. Bake for 25 minutes. Take the lid off the Dutch oven and lower heat to 450° F. Bake for another 10 to 15 minutes. Before cutting the bread, let it cool to room temperature.

84. Raspberry White Chocolate Sourdough Bread

Prep Time: 5 Hours / Cook Time: 45 Minutes / Resting Time: 8 Hours / Total Time: 13 Hours 45 Minutes / Yield: 12 slices

Ingredients:
- ¼ cup (25g) Rye flour
- ½ cups (75g) Spelt flour
- 3.15 cups / 400g Artisan bread flour
- 1 ½ cup (375g) Water
- 1 cup (120g) Raspberries
- ½ cup (87g) White chocolate chips
- 1 ¾ teaspoon (10g) salt
- ½ cup (100 g) Sourdough starter

Instructions:
1. Put bread flour, spelt flour, and rye flour in a bowl. Add the rest of the water and mix well. Let the dough rise for 30 minutes on its own.
2. Then Mix the flour and sourdough starter together.
3. Add the starter to the flour mix and stir by hand. Mix well by kneading for one to two minutes. Put the lid on and wait 30 to 60 minutes.
4. After that, add the salt. Mix the dough well, then put the lid back on top and set it aside.
5. After that, fold and stretch the dough every hour for two hours. For this, you need to grab the bottom of the dough and stretch it up and over the rest of the dough. Every time you touch the dough, do a few of these turns.
6. Raspberries and white chocolate chips should be incorporated into the dough while it is being laminated.
7. After an hour, move dough to a lightly floured surface and roll it out into a round shape. First, fold the third of the dough that is closest to you. Then, stretch the dough out to the sides. Start by folding the right side toward the center, then the left in the same way. To make a roll, fold the top of the dough inward, after that wrap the bottom of the dough over all of it. The pre-shape can be made ahead of time and left for 15 minutes. The final shape can then be made.
8. Roll this out into a circle and put it seam-side up in a proofing basket that has been well-dusted with flour.
9. After moving the dough to the Banneton, put it in the fridge overnight to rise. This cold stop will last for up to 14 hours.
10. Heat the oven to 475°F when you're ready to bake.
11. Then, take the dough out of the proofing basket, score it, and then move it to the Dutch oven. Close the lid, then put the top back on right away, and put the oven back on.
12. Lower the heat to 450°F and cook for 25 minutes.
13. After 25 minutes, take the Dutch oven's lid off and turn the pan around. For another 35 minutes, or until the crust is very caramelized, keep baking the bread.
14. Leave the oven door open and the bread inside after turning it off if you want the crust to get crunchy.
15. After taking the bread out of the oven, let the bread cool completely on your wire rack. Then, cut it into slices and serve with butter.

85. Sourdough Bread

Prep Time: 30 Minutes / Cook Time: 60 Minutes / Rise Time: 8 Hours / Total Time: 9 Hours 30 Minutes / Yield: 12 slices

Ingredients:
- 1 ½ cups (350 grams) filtered water about 100° F.
- ¼ cup (60 grams) sourdough starter (fed within the last 12-24 hours)
- 4 ¼ cups (500 grams) all-purpose flour
- 1 ½ teaspoons (9 grams) fine salt

Instructions:
1. Put the sourdough starter in a large bowl. Use a dough whisk or you can use a wooden spoon to mix in the water until it's all mixed in. Add flour and salt then mix until a shaggy dough forms. Mix the dough one last time by hand in the bowl until all the flour is gone. Put a clean, damp kitchen towel over bowl and let dough rest for about 30 to 45 minutes.
2. Dust your counter with a little flour. You can use a dough scraper or your hands to move the dough from the bowl to the counter. For 15 seconds, stretch and fold the dough. To do this, grab the edge of the dough, bring it straight up about 4 inches, and tuck it into center of the dough. Next, turn the dough by 1/4 of a turn. Do this again and again until the dough has gone around the whole circle and become tight. Put the dough back in the bowl and cover it with a damp towel or use plastic wrap if you live in a dry area). Let it rise for about 10 hours at room temperature or in a warm place (72 to 80 degrees F). Do not put the dough in the fridge. When it's fermented, the dough should look bubbly on top and below it and have doubled in size.
3. Dust your counter with a little flour. Take the dough out of the bowl and stretch and fold it again to shape it. Take a 10- to 15-minute break from the dough. Line a medium-sized bowl with a towel, or use a banneton bowl with a linen cover. Then, sprinkle a lot of flour over the bowl. For 45 to 60 minutes, let the dough rise in it.
4. Warm your oven up to 450 deg F (without the Dutch oven). Put a long piece of parchment paper over the dough bowl (about 20 inches long) and flip it over on the counter. Cut a slit in the top of the loaf with a dull or sharp sharp knife. Carefully put the dough on parchment paper into a heavy pot with a lid that fits tightly on top. NOTE: I suggest putting a round silicone sheet under the parchment paper to insulate the bottom of a Dutch oven with a dark interior. The pot can also be put on a baking sheet. This keeps the bread's bottom crust from turning too dark.
5. Cover the pot and put it in the oven. Bake the bread for about 30 minutes with the lid on. Put the lid back on and bake for 20 minutes. With oven mitts on, carefully take the bread out of the pot. If you need to, bake it right on the oven rack for around 5 to 10 minutes to make the outside crispy. You can check the bread's internal temperature to make sure it's fully cooked. It should be between 195- and 205-degrees Fahrenheit.
6. Let it cool down for at least an hour before you serve it.

86. Sourdough Bread with Flax Seeds

Prep Time: 4 days / Cook Time: 2 Hours / Total Time: 4 days 2 Hours / Yield: 16 slices

Ingredients:
- 940 g bread flour
- 192 g active sourdough starter
- water
- 92 g ground flax seed
- 142 g whole wheat flour
- 17 g sea salt

Instructions:
1. Start by making the leaven. In a large bowl or container, mix together 192 grams of active sourdough starter, 511 grams of water, 142 grams of whole wheat flour, and 340 grams of bread flour. For baking sourdough, I use a container with a lid.
2. Put a lid on top of the leaven and let it sit at room temperature until it starts to bubble a lot. Based on how warm your kitchen is and how active your starter is, this should take between 7 and 12 hours. I suggest checking on it every hour after the four-hour mark. But if you don't have much time, you can put it in the fridge overnight and continue the next day.
3. Next, put the 92 g of flax seeds and 135 g of water in a small bowl. Mix them together, then set the bowl aside.
4. When the leaven is bubbling a lot, add 150 grams of water and 600 grams of bread flour. Mix slowly by hand until everything is mixed. After that, let the dough rest for 40 minutes at room temperature so the flour can soak up the water.
5. After letting the dough rest for about 40 minutes, add 17 grams of sea salt, 50 grams of water, and the flax seeds that have been soaked. Then, use your hands to mix the dough together. Cover it and let it rest at room temperature for another 30 to 60 minutes.
6. After letting the dough rest for 30 to 60 minutes, lift the edges of the dough and fold them toward the middle to stretch and fold it. Then, put the dough in the fridge with the lid on for about 18 hours.
7. After about 18 hours, take the dough out of the fridge and let it sit for 30 minutes at room temperature. After that, roll and fold the dough. Stretch and fold dough every hour for the next two to five hours or until it is very stretchy and airy. To give you an idea, it took my dough three hours to get very stretchy and airy.
8. Then, take the dough out of the bowl or container and split it in half. Next, make each piece of dough into a tight ball by folding it four times like a book and then tucking the edges under. After shaping the loaves, let them sit on the counter for 25 minutes.
9. Next, put the loaves in bowls or bannetons so that the "seam" is facing up. I suggest that you dust your bowls or bannetons with rice flour so that the dough doesn't stick.
10. After being in the fridge for about 40 hours, heat your oven and Dutch oven to 500 degrees Fahrenheit. As soon as the Dutch oven is hot, quickly move the loaf inside. Then, cut a line across the top with a sharp knife and put the lid on top. Set the oven to 500 degrees for 25 minutes. Next, lower the heat to 460 degrees, take the Dutch oven out of the oven, and bake for another 20 to 40 minutes, until it is golden brown. Do it again for the second loaf.

87. Sourdough Maple Pecan Harvest Bread

Prep Time: 30 Minutes / Cook Time: 50 Minutes / Resting Time: 14-16 Hours / Total Time:14-16 Hours 20 Minutes / Yield: 20-24 slices

Ingredients:
- 1 cup water, between 100-115F
- 1 teaspoons salt
- 1/2 cup (120 grams) active sourdough starter
- 1 cup chopped pecans
- 1/2 cup whole wheat flour
- 1/2 teaspoon ground cinnamon
- 1/4 cup maple syrup
- 2 1/2 cups all-purpose flour
- 2 teaspoons brown sugar

Instructions:
1. Mix flour, cinnamon, brown sugar, and salt in a large bowl. Sourdough starter, maple syrup, and water should all be mixed together in a different bowl or large measuring cup. Mix until all the flour is mixed in. Then, put the dough on a floured surface and knead it until it forms a ball. Put in a bowl and let it rise for 20 minutes. This will make the dough a little flatter. Next, put pecans in the middle and use the stretch and fold method to fold them in. After taking a 30-minute break, do the folding technique four more times, for a total of two hours. After that, put the bowl in the fridge overnight with a tight lid.
2. After up to 24 hours, take the dough out of the fridge the next day and let it sit for about two hours to warm up.
3. Heat the oven to 450F and put the big Dutch oven inside with the lid on.
4. Shape your bread while the oven is getting ready. Lightly sprinkle flour on a work surface. With a spatula, carefully move the bread dough to a floured surface. Dust your hands with flour and give shape the dough into a round boule. Minimal handling is best!
5. Place the shaped dough in a well-floured proofing basket (banneton) and loosely cover it with a clean dishtowel. Flip the shaped bread over onto a piece of parchment paper right before baking. After preheating both the oven and the Dutch oven, carefully take Dutch oven out of the oven and take off the lid (carefully, as it will be very hot!). Then, use the parchment paper to lift the bread into the Dutch oven. Score the bread, spritz lightly with water, and top with a few more sunflower and pumpkin seeds. Put the pot in the oven and cover it with a lid.
6. Put the lid on your bread and bake it for 35 to 40 minutes. Then take off the lid and bake it for another 10 minutes, until the top is very brown.
7. Take the bread out of the oven and let it cool down completely before cutting it.

88. Sourdough Rosemary Bread

Prep Time: 30 Minutes / Cook Time: 40-45 Minutes / Total Time: 9 Hours 15 Minutes / Yield: 16 slices

Ingredients:
For the Levain:

- 227 grams bread flour
- 45 grams starter
- 227 grams water

Final Dough:

- 228 grams whole wheat flour
- All of the levain
- 454 grams water
- 17 grams salt
- 457 grams bread flour
- 17 to 28 grams finely chopped rosemary, depending on taste

Instructions:
1. Put the levain ingredients in a medium bowl. Mix them together, then cover the bowl using a plastic wrap and leave it at room temperature for 8 hours. You can now either use the levain right away or put it in the fridge for up to 24 hours.
2. Using a stand mixer, mix everything together except the salt and rosemary. Let it sit for 30 minutes to "autolyze."
3. Toss the dough with the rosemary and salt. Use the dough hook to work the dough for about 8 minutes.
4. In an oiled bowl, put the dough and let it rise for about two and a half hours. Every thirty minutes, fold the dough four times.
5. When the dough has doubled in size, take it out and place it on a lightly floured surface.
6. Using a bench scraper, cut the dough in half and roll each half into a ball. Put some oily plastic wrap over it and let it sit for ten minutes.
7. Use flour to dust two bannetons or floured tea towels to line two 9-inch bowls.
8. Shape boules a second time, creating a taut "skin" on outside of the dough, then place the dough, seam side up, into each basket.
9. Put oiled plastic wrap over the dough and let it rise at room temperature for about two hours, or until it gets puffy. You could also put the dough in the fridge for about 18 hours.
10. Warm up the oven to 500 degrees F and put in two Dutch ovens. If you only have single Dutch oven, you can bake one loaf at a time.
11. Take the hot Dutch ovens out of the oven and put the dough into them seam side down. Using a sharp knife or lame, make slashes in the loaves, cover, and return to the oven. Turn down the oven heat to 450 degrees F.
12. Bake with the lid on for 25 minutes and without the lid for 15 to 20 minutes. The bread should be between 205- and 210-degrees F on the inside.
13. On a wire rack, let the loaves cool all the way down.

HOLIDAYS BREADS

89. Bagel

Prep Time: 10 Minutes / Cook Time: 40 Minutes / Total Time: 50 Minutes / Yield: 12-16 slices

Ingredients:

- 1/2 tsp of Active Dry Yeast Room Temperature
- 2.5 tbsp of Everything Seasoning
- 1 - 1/2 cups Water Room Temperature
- 3 cups Flour
- 1 tsp Salt

Instructions:
1. Mix the flour, active dry yeast, and salt together in a large bowl.
2. It's time to add everything seasoning.
3. Mix the water into the mix and stir it in well.
4. Put plastic wrap over the bowl and let the dough sit for 12 to 18 hours.
5. The dough should have risen and grown after 12 to 18 hours. Warm the oven up to 450 degrees with the Dutch oven and lid inside. Before you put the dough in, the Dutch oven needs to be 450 degrees.
6. Lightly dust the Dutch oven with flour to keep the dough from sticking.
7. Put the dough in the Dutch oven. If it's sticking to your hands, sprinkle some flour on them. Put the remaining 1/2 tablespoon of everything seasoning on top of the bread.
8. Put the bread in the oven at 450 degrees and cover it with the lid. Bake for 30 minutes. No need to put the lid back on after 30 minutes. Bake for another 10 to 15 minutes, until the crust is golden brown.
9. When it's done baking, take the bread out of the Dutch oven right away so it can cool.

90. Baguette

Prep Time: 10 Minutes / Cook Time: 20 Minutes / Resting Time: 2 Hours 30 Minutes / Total Time: 3 Hours / Yield: 1 Baguette

Ingredients:

- 3 grams instant yeast (or use 4 grams active dry yeast)
- 96 grams of warm water
- 120 grams all-purpose flour
- 3 grams diamond crystal kosher salt

Instructions:

1. In a mixing bowl, mix the yeast, salt, and flour together. Along with the dry ingredients, add the water and mix until everything is well mixed. Create a sloppy, sticky ball in the bowl's bottom. Put a lid on top and wait 30 minutes.
2. The first set of folds. Grab the top edge of the dough with wet hands and pull it away from the bowl. Then fold it over the middle of the dough. Flip the bowl over three times and do it over and over. Do it twice more, and you'll have gone all the way around the dough. Turn the dough over so that the seam side is now facing down. Keep it covered and rest for 30 minutes.
3. The second set of folds. Go all the way around the bowl and fold the same way you did before. Turn the dough over so that the seam side is facing down. Put something over it and rest for an hour. If you let it, the dough will double or triple in size and get foamy and airy.
4. At the end of the hour, put a Dutch oven with a lid inside and heat the oven to 450°F.
5. Making shape. Put some flour on top of the dough in the bowl, and then take it out and place it on a lightly floured surface. Add a little flour to the top of the dough, just enough to keep it from sticking to your hands. Stretch dough out into a rectangle shape, with the long side facing you.
6. You can seal the edge with the heel of your hand or your fingertips after folding down the top third of the dough. You can turn the dough around so that the folded edge is now the side that is closest to you. Once more, fold the top third of the dough down and seal the edge. Finally, fold the dough in half by bringing the two edges together against the counter and folding the top edge down.
7. As you work your way through the folding process, the dough will naturally stretch out. If you need to, add more flour to keep it from sticking to your hands.
8. Tapering. Roll the dough forward so that the seam is underneath. Spread the dough out evenly by rolling it out quickly from the middle. Then, roll the ends so that your pinkies are against the counter while you bend your hands to the side.
9. In order for the baguette to fit inside your Dutch oven or other baking vessel, make sure it's not longer than that.
10. Last rest. Sprinkle flour on a clean kitchen towel and carefully move the baguette onto it. Pinch the towel so that it can stands up on both sides of the baguette's length. This will keep it in shape. (Optional) Use binder clips to hold the towel in place loosely so that the baguette has room to rise and expand. To keep the baguette from drying out, wrap it in plastic wrap or put it in a big plastic bag.
11. While the oven heats up, let it rise for 30 minutes.
12. Heat your oven to 450°F and put a Dutch oven inside with the lid on. Grab your lame and a small spray bottle of water. Make sure there is room for the Dutch oven when you take it out to put the baguette inside.
13. A score. Put the baguette on a half sheet of parchment paper so it lies on its side, corner to corner, and gently roll it up with the dish towel. Along the length of the baguette, make scores going up and down. Spray the loaf with water all over quickly, then put it in the hot Dutch oven, spray it with more water, and cover it right away.
14. Bake. Cover and bake for 10 minutes. After 10 minutes, take the lid off and bake for another 10 minutes. If your baguette needs a little more color, bake it for another 2 to 3 minutes directly on the rack.
15. Once the loaf is done, move it to a cooling rack and let the bagutte cool completely before cutting it.

91. Braided Saffron Challah Bread

Prep Time: 30 Mins / Cook Time: 50 Mins / Rising Time: 2 Hours 20 Mins / Total Time: 3 Hour 40 Mins / Yield: 8 slices

Ingredients:

- 3 1/2 cups all-purpose flour
- 1 cup lukewarm water
- 4 tbsp (1/2 stick) of unsalted butter melted
- Pinch saffron threads
- 3 large eggs divided
- 1 1/2 tsp active dry yeast
- 1/4 cup sugar
- 1 tbsp olive oil
- 1 large egg yolk
- 1 1/2 tsp salt
- 1 tbsp water

Instructions:

1. Mix the warm water, sugar, yeast, and saffron together in a medium-sized bowl. Allow mixture sit for about 15 minutes or until it appears foamy, which means the yeast is working. Add salt, melted butter, two eggs, and egg yolk to the yeast mixture and mix it well. Combine the flour slowly while mixing it in to make a soft, sticky dough. Apply flour to a work surface and then move the dough to it. Knead the dough for about 10 mins, adding up to an extra cup of flour at a time, if needed, until it is smooth and elastic. Apply olive oil to a medium-sized bowl, then put the dough inside and turn it to coat it with the oil. Leave the bowl with the dough covered with a proper clean kitchen towel in a warm place for an hour, or until it has doubled in size.
2. Fold and turn the dough. Cover the bowl again, then let the dough rise for 1 hour. This time, let it double in size.
3. Warm the oven to 350°F. To make a braid, cut the dough into three equal pieces. For each piece, roll it into a 2-by-20-inch rope. Pinch the ropes together at the top, then braid the dough, weaving the strands together to make the loaf. Place parchment paper around the edges of a Dutch oven and place the braided loaf inside, making sure it fits the shape of the Dutch oven. Insert the lid onto the pot and let the dough rise for twenty minutes, or until it has doubled in size.
4. Take the lid off the pot and set it on the middle rack. The bread should be baked for 40 minutes or until the internal temperature reaches between 190°F and 205°F. When you tap the bread, it should sound hollow. Mix the last egg and water in a small bowl with a whisk to make an egg wash. Apply the egg wash to the bread, then bake for another 5 to 10 minutes. Before slicing, let the bread cool all the way down.

92. Coconut & Lime Brioche Buns

Prep Time: 30 Minutes / Cook Time: 60 Minutes / Raising Time: 1 Hour / Total Time: 2 Hours 30 Minutes / Yield: 9 Buns

Ingredients:
Brioche Dough:

- 1 ¼ tsp (1/2 packet) instant dry active yeast
- ¼ tsp sea salt
- 2 tbsp organic cane sugar
- 2 ¼ + ¼ cups all-purpose flour, divided
- 1 tsp lime zest
- Unsalted vegan butter, for greasing
- 1 ¼ cup of warm full fat coconut milk (at about 120°F)

Coconut & Lime Filling:

- ¼ cup coconut butter in liquid form
- 1 tbsp lime juice
- ¼ cup organic cane sugar
- 1 tsp lime zest

Cream Cheese Icing:

- 3 tbsp powdered sugar
- ⅛ tsp coconut extract, optional but recommended
- ½ tsp lime zest
- ¼ cup vegan cream cheese, at room temperature
- 1 tsp lime juice
- Unsweetened shredded coconut, for garnish

Instructions:

1. In a large bowl, mix coconut milk and sugar together with a whisk. Lay the yeast on top and wait 5 minutes for it to rise. Use a wooden spoon to mix.
2. Put a clean towel over it and let it rise in a warm place for an hour.
3. While dough is rising, mix the ingredients for the Coconut and lime Filling in a bowl right before you use them. Set aside.
4. After an hour, use your wooden spoon to mix in last 1/4 cup of flour.
5. Now, dust a clean surface with flour and put the dough on it. You may need to add a little more flour if your dough starts to stick to the surface. Knead the dough for about 5 minutes.
6. When you roll out the dough, it should be about 12 inches by 16 inches.
7. With a silicone spatula, spread the Coconut and lime Filling out on the dough, leaving 1/2 inch of space around the edges.
8. Form a tight log. Lay the seam down.
9. Prepare the Dutch oven by greasing it and then cut 9 to 10 buns into pieces that are 1 1/2 inches thick. Put the lid on top of the Dutch oven.

10. Preheat your oven to 350 degrees Fahrenheit and bake the brioche buns for 30 minutes with the lid on.
11. During this time, make the cream cheese icing by mixing all of its parts in a bowl until the icing is smooth. Set aside.
12. Take off the lid of the Dutch oven after 30 minutes of baking and bake without it for another 30 minutes, or until golden.
13. After taking the brioches out of the oven, let them cool for 15 minutes. Then, put some cream cheese frosting and shredded coconut on top of them.

93. Cornbread with Green Chiles

Prep Time: 5 Minutes / Cook Time: 20 Minutes / Total Time: 25 Minutes / Yield: 6 slices

Ingredients:
- 1 cup milk
- 1 teaspoon salt
- ½ cup flour
- 1 tablespoon baking powder
- 2 tablespoons butter
- 1 egg
- 2 tablespoons honey
- 1 (4 oz) can green chiles, drained
- 1 cup cornmeal
- ¼ cup shredded cheddar cheese

Instructions:
1. Use 24 charcoal briquettes or a campfire to light the wood embers.
2. Put the milk, egg, and honey in a bowl and beat them together. Combine cornmeal, baking powder, flour and salt, which are the dry ingredients.
3. Arrange 7 of the charcoals or embers in a ring and place the Dutch oven on top. Put the butter in when it's hot and let it melt. Place the cornmeal batter in the pan after the butter has melted. Add the cheese and green chiles on top.
4. Place the 17 remaining charcoals or embers on top of the lid of the Dutch oven to heat it up to about 425 degrees. Place the cornbread in the oven and cook for 20 minutes, or until the center is fully cooked and the top starts to turn brown.
5. Remove carefully from the heat, serve, and enjoy!

94. Eggnog Bread

Prep Time: 15 Minutes / Cook Time: 50-55 Minutes / Resting Time: 1 Hour 30 Minutes / Total Time: 2 Hours 40 Minutes / Yield: 12-16 slices

Ingredients:
- ¼ teaspoon Cinnamon
- ¾ teaspoons Baking Soda
- 1 teaspoon Vanilla Extract
- ¼ teaspoon Nutmeg
- 1 ½ cups Eggnog
- ½ teaspoon Baking Powder
- ¼ teaspoon Salt
- 1 Egg
- 4 Tablespoons Softened butter
- 1 ½ cups Flour
- ½ Cup Sugar

Eggnog Glaze:
- 1 Tablespoon Eggnog
- 1 Tablespoon Melted Butter
- ¾ Cup Powdered Sugar

Instructions:
1. Heat your 10" Dutch oven to 375 degrees and butter it well. 13 briquettes on top and 8 on the bottom.
2. Prepare eggnog bread by mixing flour, baking soda, baking powder, cinnamon, nutmeg and salt in a medium-sized bowl.
3. Combine the butter and sugar in a different medium-sized bowl. Mix with an electric mixer until smooth, stopping to scrape the bowl occasionally. Mix the egg and vanilla in until the mixture is smooth.
4. Simply mix about ½ of the flour mixture into the butter mixture. Incorporate eggnog and mix well. Mix in rest of flour mixture until you have a smooth batter.
5. Place batter in Dutch oven and bake for about 50 to 55 minutes, or you need to wait until a toothpick inserted into the middle comes out clean. You could take out the 10" aluminum liner to let it cool. Give it about an hour and a half to cool down.
6. Get the eggnog glaze ready by: Combine eggnog, butter, and powdered sugar in a small bowl. Layer it on top of the bread. For best results, serve right away or wait about 15 minutes for the frosting to set.

95. Naan

Prep Time: 1 Hour 10 Minutes / Cook Time: 10 Minutes / Total Time: 1 Hour 20 Minutes / Yield: 8-10 naan

Ingredients:
- ¾ cup of warm milk not hot, I use whole milk
- 2-3 tablespoons of melted butter for brushing or olive oil
- 1 ½ teaspoons baking powder aluminum free
- ¼ teaspoon kosher salt plus more for sprinkling
- ¾ teaspoon active dry yeast
- ¼ cup of hot water not boiling, from your tap
- 1 teaspoon baking soda
- 1 cup of plain Greek yogurt
- 4 cups all-purpose flour
- 1 tablespoon sugar all-natural cane sugar
- Fresh cilantro parsley or other herbs for sprinkling

Instructions:
1. Mix the sugar and yeast (yeast LOVES sugar, but not metal) in a glass or ceramic mixing bowl. Pour in your hot (not boiling) water and stir it slowly until the yeast and sugar are mixed in. Let it sit for about 5 to 10 minutes until it foams up and rises a bit. It should smell like yeasty or bread.
2. Warm up the milk in a small saucepan. Do not make it hot or boil it, because you do not want to kill the yeast. It should be warm to the touch. When your yeast smells like yeast, add flour, yogurt, warm milk, baking powder, baking soda, and salt. Use a wooden spoon to stir it around until it forms a sticky ball. Place in a warm area for an hour and cover with oil-sprayed plastic wrap or a damp tea towel.
3. Once the dough has risen, make a disc out of it and use a knife or a bench scraper to cut it into eight or ten roughly equal pieces. They don't have to be perfect; in fact, that makes the bread look more rough. Roll out each dough ball one at a time on a lightly floured surface into a flat bread that is about 6 to 8 inches wide and not too thin. Do it again with the rest of the dough.
4. Set Dutch oven on medium-high heat and heat it up until it's hot. Melt butter or oil and brush it on both sides of the naan dough. Put some other spices on top too, like garlic, cumin, or paprika.
5. Put a piece of naan in the hot pan at a time and cover it with a lid. Bake for one minute, or until bubbles start to form. To make the other side golden, flip it over and bake for another minute or two. Take it off the heat and, if you want, brush it with a little more butter and sprinkle it with kosher salt and chopped fresh parsley or cilantro. To keep the naan warm, put it in a dish or basket lined with cloth.

96. No Knead Cinnamon Swirl Bread

Prep Time: 20 Minutes / Cook Time: 45 Minutes / Resting Time: 2 Hours 15 Minutes / Total Time: 3 Hours 20 Minutes / Yield: 8 slices

Ingredients:
Bread:
- 3 cups flour
- 1 1/4 teaspoon salt
- 1 5/8 cup water
- 1/4 teaspoon instant yeast

Filling:
- 1 tablespoon cinnamon
- 2 tablespoons unsalted butter
- 1/2 cup sugar

Instructions:
1. Put the yeast, salt, and flour in a large bowl and mix them together. Mix the dough with water until it forms a sticky mass. Put plastic wrap over it and let it sit for 12 to 18 hours. Longer is better. Place the dough on a lightly floured surface and fold it over itself a few times. Put a thin cloth over it and let it rest for 15 minutes.
2. Make the cinnamon sugar filling while you wait. Take a small saucepan, melt the butter over medium heat. Take it off the heat and mix in the sugar and cinnamon.
3. On a floured surface, stretch the dough into a 16-by-8-inch rectangle. Spread cinnamon filling over the entire surface. Simply roll up the long edge like a cinnamon roll. Then, roll the tube into a round loaf shape. Tuck the end into the middle to make it look like a knot. Sprinkle some flour on a thin piece of cloth and put the loaf on top of it. Cover the cloth with it. Let it rise for two hours.
4. Preheat the oven and a 6 to 8-quart Dutch oven to 450 degrees for about 30 minutes before the dough is done rising. Take care to open the cloth up and put the bread in the Dutch oven. Put a lid on it and bake for about 30 minutes. Take off the lid and, then bake for another 10 to 15 minutes to make the top brown. Cool it before serves.

97. Olive Oil and Rosemary No Knead Bread

Prep Time: 11 Hours / Cook Time: 45 Minutes / Total Time: 11 Hours 45 Minutes / Yield: 8 slices

Ingredients:
- 1 1/4 cups room temperature water
- 1/2 tsp instant yeast
- 1 1/2 tsp table salt
- 15 oz (3 cups) all-purpose flour
- 2-3 tbsp chopped fresh rosemary
- 1/4 cup olive oil

Instructions:
1. Put the yeast, salt, rosemary, and flour in a large bowl and mix them together. Put in the olive oil and water, and use a big spoon to mix the flour in completely. You might have to use your hands to mix in the flour all the way. It will be sticky and wet. Put the bowl somewhere warm in the kitchen and wrap it in plastic wrap. Leave it there for 10 to 12 hours.
2. The dough is ready to be shaped when it has bubbles all over it and looks puffy.
3. Put a little flour on the work surface and add a little more flour on top of the dough. Scrape the dough out of bowl and onto the floured surface with your fingertips. Just fold the dough over a few times to make it more structure. After that, roll the dough into a ball. Use oil to cover a piece of parchment paper. Cover dough with a damp kitchen towel after putting it on the parchment. You should let the dough rest for an hour.
4. Preheat the oven to 500F and put a Dutch oven pot with a lid in it 30 minutes before you want to bake the bread.
5. If you want to bake the bread, you can either use a serrated knife to cut a slit in the top or grease another piece of parchment paper and flip the bread onto it so that the seam side is facing up. Either way, the bread will be able to rise while it's baking.
6. Then, hold the bread by the edges of the parchment paper and put it into the big Dutch oven pot. Put the pot back in the oven with the lid on top. Turn down the heat to 425F. Put the bread in the oven for two hours.
7. Take off the lid and bake for 15 more minutes. Put the bread on a rack to cool down.

98. Panettone

Prep Time: 45 Minutes / Cook Time: 40 Minutes / Rising Time: 1 Days / Total Time: 1 Day 1 Hour 25 Minutes / Yield: 1 (7 inch) Panettone

Ingredients:
For the Panettone Starter:
- ¼ cup sourdough starter
- ¼ cup cold water
- ½ cup all-purpose flour

For the Dried Fruit:
- ¼ cup rum
- ½ cup diced dried pineapple
- ½ cup golden raisins
- ½ cup dried cherries, quartered

For the Dough:
- 2 ½ cups all-purpose flour
- 1 tablespoon freshly grated lemon zest
- 1 ½ teaspoons vanilla extract
- ¼ cup warm water
- 2 large eggs
- 6 tablespoons butter, at room temperature
- 1 ¼ teaspoons fine salt
- 2 tablespoons white sugar
- 1 tablespoon freshly grated orange zest
- ⅓ cup white sugar
- 1 (.25 ounce) package active dry yeast

For Egg Wash:
- 1 large egg
- 1 tablespoon water

Instructions:
1. In a bowl, mix flour, cold water, and sourdough starter the day before you bake. Leave it out at room temperature for 8 hours to overnight with the lid on.
2. In a different bowl, mix the pineapple, cherries, and raisins at the same time. Add the rum and stir. Allow fruit to soak, tossing occasionally, for 8 hours to overnight.
3. Put warm water into the stand mixer's large bowl that has a dough hook attached to it. Put in the yeast and wait 10 minutes for it to dissolve. To the bowl, add the orange zest, lemon zest, eggs, vanilla extract, and 1/3 cup plus 2 tablespoons of sugar. Mix everything together. Place the panettone starter in a bowl. Mix in the flour and salt.
4. For about 10 minutes, knead the dough until it is very smooth and springy. Stop and clean the sides if needed. Add the butter and knead dough for about 5 minutes, or until the butter is fully mixed in and the

dough is soft and a little sticky. Move to the surface of your work.
5. Use wet fingers and a bench scraper to toss and fold the dough into a rough ball shape. Put the dough back in the bowl. Let it rise for about three hours, covered, until it has doubled in size.
6. Put the dough back on your work surface and roll it into a rough ball. Put into a plastic bag that can be closed again. Put in the fridge for 8 hours to overnight.
7. Take the dough out of the bag and stretch it out into a rectangle shape. Put some flour on it and roll it out until it's at least 1/2 inch thick. Cover the whole thing with the dried fruit. Make a log out of the dough to keep the fruit inside. Make a ball out of the log by rolling both ends toward the middle.
8. Insert a short, wide piece of paper panettone mold into the dough ball. Let the dough rise for three to four hours, or until it comes at least two thirds of the way up the sides. Cover with plastic wrap.
9. Turn the oven on to 350 degrees F (175 degrees C).
10. Using a pastry brush, spread the egg and water mixture over the panettone. On top, make two crosswise slits.
11. In a hot oven, bake for about 40 to 45 minutes, or until the top is nicely browned. Poke two skewers through the panettone on each side. Then, turn it over so that it forms a panettone hole or a Dutch oven. Turn it over and let it cool for two hours.
12. Take the sticks out and cut them into pieces.

99. Pita Bread

Prep Time: 25 Minutes / Cook Time: 05 Minutes / Raising Time: 1 Hour / Total Time: 1 Hour 30 Minutes / Yield: 6

Ingredients:
- 1/2 cup whole wheat flour
- 1/2 teaspoon salt mixed with 1/2-tsp. water
- 1 cup tepid water (110°-115°F)
- 1/2 cup all-purpose flour
- 2 cups all-purpose flour
- 1 package dry, quick action yeast

Instructions:
1. First, add yeast to 1 cup of water and stir it around. Put in 2 cups of flour along with the salt and water mix. Combine well.
2. Mix in the all-purpose flour and wheat until the mixture is smooth. If it gets too dry, add a little water. Let it rise until it's about twice as big, then cut it into six pieces. Now, roll each piece into a ball and then into a flat round that is about ¼" thick.
3. Put it on the bottom of a 550°F Dutch oven and bake for 5 minutes, or until it's just barely grown. Take the cake out of the oven and let it cool on a rack.

100. Rosca de Reyes

Prep Time: 40 Minutes / Cook Time: 15 Minutes / Resting Time: 2 Hours / Total Time: 2 Hours 55 Minutes / Yield: 2 loaves

Ingredients:

For yeast sponge:

- 3/4 cup all-purpose flour
- pinch of sugar
- 2 1/4 teaspoons active dry yeast
- 1/2 cup warm water

For dough:

- 3 cups all-purpose flour
- 4 large eggs
- 1/3 cup sugar
- 1 1/2 tsp brandy
- 1 1/2 cup mixture of candied & dried fruit (candied orange and lemon peel, cranberries and apricots)
- zest of 1 orange or lemon
- rice flour
- 1 1/2 tsp vanilla extract
- 1/2 cup unsalted butter
- olive oil for greasing
- 1/2 tsp salt

For decoration:

- blanched whole almonds
- not-reconstituted dried fruit
- two egg yolks, lightly beaten

Instructions:

1. First, make sure the eggs and butter are at room temperature.
2. Put the dried fruit in a cup, and then add hot water to cover it. Set it aside after draining.
3. Combine your yeast, sugar, and warm water in a two-cup measuring cup. Stir the ingredients together. Once it starts to foam, add the flour and mix it in. Cover with your plastic wrap and let it sit for about 20 minutes, or until the sponge is almost 2 cups full.
4. If the paddle on your stand mixer rests on the bottom of the bowl, beat the butter and sugar for five minutes until they are light and fluffy. If not, relax with a whisk (like we did). Combine the zest and salt and beat until nicely mixed.
5. Now add the eggs one at a time, mixing well after each one. Relax, my dough did not seem to be coming together at this point. Add the yeast sponge now and beat until everything is well mixed. Mix in two cups of flour on low speed. Combine the last cup of flour, the last egg, the brandy, and the vanilla. Mix on low speed until the mixture is smooth.
6. Turn up the speed to medium and beat the dough until it is smooth and stretchy. In this step, add your reconstituted fruit and mix on low speed until it's all mixed in.
7. Prepare a big bowl by greasing it and washing your hands. Create a ball of dough and put it in the bowl. Place a plastic wrap over it and let it sit for about an hour, or until it doubles in size.
8. Combine two pieces of parchment paper with rice flour. Create two balls out of the dough. You can make a ring by carefully poking a hole in the middle and shaping it. Wrap the ring in greased plastic wrap and place it on the parchment paper. Allow to rise again for one hour.
9. Heat the oven up to 400 degrees. Remove one of the loaves from the plastic wrap and top it with dried fruit and almonds. Spread egg yolk all over the top until it's sealed.
10. Put the baking sheet with parchment paper on top of it and then into the oven. On the other hand, flip your Dutch oven over and use it to cover the dough. Put it in the oven for 15 minutes.
11. Take the Dutch oven out of the oven and lower the heat to 330 degrees. Bake until golden brown, then take out and cool on racks. Put on the other ring and do it again.

Made in United States
Troutdale, OR
01/11/2024